BRISTOL AND GLOUCESTERSHIRE AEROSPACE INDUSTRY

BRISTOL AND GLOUCESTERSHIRE AEROSPACE INDUSTRY

Steph Gillett

AMBERLEY

For my parents.

Front cover image: Former Gulf Air and East African VC10 airliners being converted into aerial refuelling tankers for the RAF at Filton in the 1980s. (Reproduced under licence from and courtesy of BAE SYSTEMS)

First published 2017

Amberley Publishing
The Hill, Stroud
Gloucestershire, GL5 4EP

www.amberley-books.com

British Library Cataloguing in Publication Data.
A catalogue record for this book is available from the British Library.

ISBN 978 1 4456 6332 6 (print)
ISBN 978 1 4456 6333 3 (ebook)

Typeset in 10.5pt on 13pt Sabon.
Typesetting and Origination by Amberley Publishing.
Printed in the UK.

Contents

Gloster aircraft passing Flamborough Head, Yorkshire: Javelin F(AW) Mk 4 XA735, Meteor NF14 WS724, and Gladiator L8032. (Jet Age Museum/Russell Adams collection)

Foreword

Growing up in north Bristol in the 1960s, I was very conscious of the airfield at Filton. Although not living within sight of the aircraft works, we were certainly in earshot. The noise from jet engines being put through their paces was sometimes dramatic; so too was the occasional sight (and sound) of a Vulcan V-bomber rising apparently vertically on the horizon. Many aircraft also passed overhead, some flights no doubt connected with Filton. I failed to confirm the identity of many of these, even with the aid of my *I-Spy Aircraft* book, but the RAF's Series 252 Britannia turboprop XN404 was certainly one of them; I have photographic evidence.

Seeing Concorde 002 on its maiden flight in 1969, albeit briefly from our back garden, felt in many ways more significant than the Apollo moon landing later that year. Experiencing the not quite shattering effect of a sonic boom on the windows of my school was definitely more tangible! The year before Concorde's first flight, a family outing with neighbours to an air show at Filton provided my first view of a Pegasus-powered Harrier jump jet. The displays also featured other aircraft representing the products of Bristol and Gloster, and I am pleased to include some of my late father's photographs from the event among the pages that follow. Incidentally, my father was nearly nine years old when he witnessed the crash of the prototype Bristol Type 133 monoplane at Longwell Green, near Bristol, in 1935. Unlike other boys from his school, he failed to claim a piece of silver fabric covering as a souvenir.

An aborted engineering course at Filton Technical College in 1972 was a missed opportunity to take more notice of the airfield and factories. Two decades on from then and my employment as a community worker in Yate made me aware of the Parnall story for the first time. My later role as museums officer for South Gloucestershire gave me a much deeper understanding of the region's aviation heritage. I was able to support two successful local initiatives, to have First World War hangars at Patchway and 'new' Filton House (now Pegasus House) protected by formal listing. In a subsequent role I had the honour to provide curatorial support to both the Bristol Aero Collection (then at Kemble Airfield) and Gloucestershire Aviation Collection.

During my time in South Gloucestershire I undertook a postgraduate course in industrial heritage, and for my dissertation chose to research the aviation industry of Bristol and Gloucestershire. This focussed on the development of the various manufacturers and dealt more with factory structures than aircraft. I have revisited and updated the study to include more about the many products of the aerospace companies, but this is *not* an aeroplane book (or an aero-engine book). The story begins with the first and largest establishment, which is dealt with in a broadly chronological way. Although most of the Filton and Patchway sites are in historic Gloucestershire, and outside the city, the industry has long been associated with Bristol (the Brabazon Hangar is within the city boundary). The narrative then moves north, via Parnall, to Gloster, and ends with some of Gloucestershire's important component suppliers. The mergers, demergers, multinationals, consortia and name changes (not to mention the alphabet soup of abbreviations and acronyms) can make it rather difficult to follow the fortunes of individual companies, especially during the past two decades; I hope I have done nothing to confuse or mislead in this respect. Where I have used 'Bristol', 'Gloster', etc., please assume this means the company of that name, unless it obviously doesn't.

In November 2003 I joined thousands of others in the wind and rain at Filton airfield to witness the last flight home of Concorde 216. Much more recently I have had the privilege to undertake some research for the new Aerospace Bristol museum that is now home to this, the last Concorde built. I am sure the book will have benefited from this involvement. No doubt I will have omitted things some will feel should have been included, or given too much space to other aspects; certainly, there is much more that could have been included than there is space in this book.

The worldwide influence of the region's aerospace industry was brought home to me a few years ago when I journeyed to south-east Asia. Of the five flights to and within three countries, each one was made in an Airbus product; I was almost certainly flying on wings developed at Filton.

I hope you enjoy reading this book at least as much as I have enjoyed writing it.

Steph Gillett

June 2017

Chapter 1

Bristol Aircraft

The British & Colonial Aeroplane Co.

The British & Colonial Aeroplane Co. (BCAC) was one of the first aeroplane constructors when it established its factory at Filton in 1910 and provided the beginnings of an aerospace industry that continues to flourish near Bristol a century and more later. The company was formed by Sir George White (1854–1916), having become convinced of the potential for aviation after watching the Wright brothers flying in France in 1909. White was, among other things, the chairman of Bristol Tramways & Carriage Co., and it was to the shareholders of this company that he promoted his plans in February 1910.

The BCAC was registered with a capital of £25,000 (equivalent to around £2.725 million in 2017), substantially more than that of the other pioneer aircraft manufacturers Handley Page and Short Brothers. White registered three other companies at the same time: Bristol Aeroplane, Bristol Aviation, and British & Colonial Aviation, each with a nominal capital of £100. The first board members of BCAC were Sir George himself, his brother Samuel (1861–1928), his son (George) Stanley (1883–1964), and his nephews Henry White Smith (1879–1944) and Sydney Ernest Smith (1881–1943).

White set up his aircraft works in two iron sheds at the top of Homestead Road in Filton, which he leased from the Tramways Company. The sheds had been built as a bus depot and bus chassis manufacturing works in 1908; they survived in a much-modified form until the end of the twentieth century. The company headquarters were at Clare Street House, Bristol.

To get the business moving quickly, BCAC intended to produce aeroplanes under licence from the French manufacturer Société Zodiac and a biplane designed by Gabriel Voisin (1880–1973) was obtained, but despite its excellent finish, the aircraft proved to be too heavy and underpowered and incapable of flight when tested at Brooklands, Surrey. The five Bristol-Zodiacs then under construction at Filton were scrapped and BCAC successfully sued Zodiac for compensation. In June 1910, the company began designing an aeroplane of its own, the Bristol Biplane, using

In this early view of the British & Colonial Aeroplane Company's works in Homestead Road at Filton, an incomplete aircraft and components can be glimpsed through the open doors. (Reproduced under licence from and courtesy of BAE SYSTEMS)

drawings prepared by the works manager George H. Challenger (1881–1947). Challenger had been an engineer with the Tramways Company, where his father was general manager. This aeroplane was essentially a copy of a successful design by Henri Farman (1874–1958), but with improved metal fittings as used on the Zodiac.

The Boxkite, as it is more widely known, was powered by a pusher engine, with the propeller behind the pilot facing backwards. With no engine production facility of their own, the very successful Gnome seven-cylinder 'Omega' rotary engine of 50 hp (37.3 kW) was used. This French engine, developed by the Seguin brothers, was the world's first production rotary engine and some 4,000 Gnomes had been sold by the start of the First World War. White secured the selling rights for the Gnome in Britain and its then colonies.

The Boxkite was piloted on its first flight by Frenchman Maurice Edmond at Larkhill, on Salisbury Plain, at the end of July 1910. In November, fellow French pilots Henri Jullerot and Maurice Tétard demonstrated the aeroplane in front of a large crowd on Durdham Down, Bristol, reaching a height of 100 ft (30.4 m).

Despite its ungainly appearance the Boxkite was a success and two a week were being produced by the end of 1910. A total of seventy-eight Boxkites were ultimately constructed, gaining a reputation as a sporting and training aeroplane, including sixty of an extended military model first ordered by the War Office in March 1911.

A replica Boxkite can be seen in the front hall of Bristol Museum & Art Gallery, one of three built from the original drawings by Miles & Co. for the 1965 film *Those Magnificent Men in Their Flying Machines*, where it featured as the *Phoenix Flyer*. After filming the aeroplane was sold by 20th Century Fox to the British Aircraft Corporation at Filton, and subsequently presented to the Museum.

Early in 1911 the works at Filton were enlarged so that five aircraft could be laid out at the same time. During the first year of production over 100 aeroplanes were built by BCAC's workforce of eighty, including its first monoplane, designed by Challenger and Archibald Low (1878–1969), who both later moved to Vickers Ltd. Engine test runs in the early days were carried out by the rudimentary method of tying the aeroplane to a convenient flagpole or iron railings to prevent it taking flight.

The experienced pilot and engineer Pierre Prier (1886–1950) was invited to join BCAC as a monoplane designer soon after completing the first non-stop flight from

As well as seeing service with the RFC, Bristol Boxkite aeroplanes were supplied to the Imperial Russian Air Service and Australian Flying Corps. Boxkite No. 12 was specially prepared for a mission to India in January 1911. Its first flights in Calcutta were watched by a crowd of 100,000. (Reproduced under licence from and courtesy of BAE SYSTEMS)

In this early view inside the original erecting hall, carpenters are preparing and assembling aeroplane components including wing spars. In the foreground a range of hand tools includes wood planes and chisels of various sizes. (Reproduced under licence from and courtesy of BAE SYSTEMS)

London to Paris in April 1911. Prier set about designing a single-seat monoplane to compete in the annual Gordon Bennett Cup race the following month. It was not possible to complete the aircraft in time but it led to a series of successful military and training monoplanes, of which thirty-four were completed before the end of 1912, by which time Prier had left the company.

E. C. Gordon England (1891–1976) joined BCAC as a staff pilot in 1911, but his aptitude for aircraft design was recognised when he converted an earlier Challenger Type T biplane from pusher to tractor configuration; this became known as the Challenger-England. Following this conversion, England designed the G.E. series of biplanes, five in total, of which the G.E.2 version was entered in the military aeroplane trials at Larkhill in August 1912. But the G.E. design was abandoned and England resigned in the spring of 1913.

Another BCAC aeroplane entered in the Larkhill trials of 1912 was a monoplane designed by Henri Coandă(1886–1972), a Romanian engineer and inventor. Coandă joined the company in January 1912 to develop and improve the Prier monoplanes and was responsible for overall design policy until his return to Romania in October 1914.

Filton House was taken over by the aeroplane company in August 1911 and used as offices. The House was granted Grade II listed status in September 1952, some fifteen months after this photograph was taken. The ornamental gates were added to the listing in 1984. (Reproduced under licence from and courtesy of BAE SYSTEMS)

Filton House, probably built in the first quarter of the eighteenth century, had been a farmhouse and a private residence before being acquired by Bristol Tramways in August 1911. It was first leased to BCAC as offices and then sold to the company in April 1912, and heavily restored in the mid-twentieth century. Cottages built around 1900 in Fairlawn Avenue as accommodation for tramway staff were used by the aeroplane company as both offices and accommodation until 1976, and then for administration until they were demolished in around 1990. By the end of 1911, the company's capital had been increased to £100,000.

An important staff appointment in 1911 was that of Frank Barnwell (1880–1938), who joined the company as a draughtsman, having served an apprenticeship with a shipbuilding company. Frank and his brother Harold (1878–1917) designed and built three experimental aircraft between 1908 and 1910. Barnwell would later become chief aircraft designer (1915–1921 and 1923–1936) and chief engineer (1936–1938).

In December 1911, a secret design office was set up in No. 4 Fairlawn Avenue, where Barnwell and his soon-to-be-appointed assistant, Clifford Tinson (1890–1982),

The physical laboratory of the engine division is seen here in 1928. Equipment includes a Buckton 560-lb testing machine dated 1917. Joshua Buckton & Co. Ltd was a machine tool manufacturer based at Wellhouse Foundry in Leeds. In front of this is an Izod patent impact tester made by W. & T. Avery Ltd of Birmingham. (Courtesy of Rolls-Royce Heritage Trust)

were tasked to work with naval officer Charles Dennistoun Burney (1888–1968) on his novel proposals for seaplanes. Barnwell worked only on Burney's ideas, which included using a hydrofoil undercarriage, until the end of 1913, during which time the X.2 and X.3 prototypes had been built. But they were not very successful and when Admiralty funding for further trials was not forthcoming the programme was abandoned in July 1914. Burney went on to develop the Paravane mine-sweeping device – effectively an underwater kite.

First World War

Bristol had success with monoplane designs, but fatal failures of single-wing aircraft (including the crash of one of the Bristol-Coandă Monoplanes in September 1912) led the Royal Flying Corps (RFC) to reject monoplanes, despite remaining popular in mainland Europe. Their ban led BCAC to accepting a series of contracts to build Royal Aircraft Factory-designed B.E.2 single-engine two-seat biplanes for the War Office. Variants of B.E.2 aircraft flew with the RFC (later RAF) from 1912 until the end of the First World War. The works at Filton were expanded to cope with this work for which capital was yet again increased in 1913 to £250,000. The outbreak of the First World War in July 1914 led to increased demands for aircraft and continuing expansion of the factory and a new airfield, spreading across more fields. By August 1914, BCAC had produced a total of 260 aeroplanes.

With a lull in work on the Burney flying boats, Barnwell was permitted to convert an unfinished Coandă monoplane fuselage into a high-speed biplane, which he designed in collaboration with test pilot Harry Busteed (1887–1965) during the second half of 1913. Busteed had arrived from Australia in 1911 together with the future co-founder of Hawker Aircraft, Harry Hawker (1889–1921), among others. The resulting Baby

Operators pose among their belt-driven lathes in the machine shop in 1918. Women were recruited to all sections of the works during the First World War to cover vacancies caused by men leaving to serve in the armed forces. Some of the lathes seen are American-built Lodge & Shipley machines. (Reproduced under licence from and courtesy of BAE SYSTEMS)

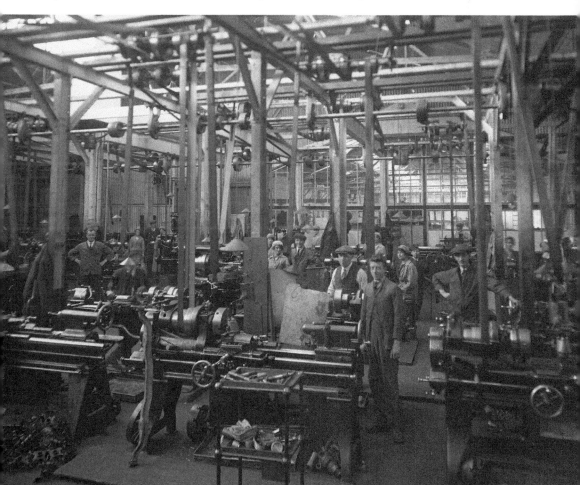

Biplane, which became the prototype Scout A, first flew in February 1914 and was entered for several races that year. It was lost in the English Channel during the return leg of the London–Paris–London race due to incomplete refuelling in France; the pilot was rescued. Two almost-identical Scout Bs were completed in August 1914 and immediately requisitioned by the War Office. Impressed by their speed and climbing ability, the War Office and Admiralty both ordered production versions – the Scout C, of which 161 were built. Many Scout Cs were constructed by Bristol Tramways at their Brislington depot as Filton was committed to B.E.2c production.

Barnwell was enlisted as a pilot with the RFC at the beginning of the First World War but was released from active service in August 1915 and returned to BCAC in his role as chief designer, where he remedied some earlier problems with the Scout C. The revised Scout D was completed in November 1915 and 210 of this version were produced – 130 for the RFC and 80 for the Royal Naval Air Service (RNAS). In 1923 Barnwell reviewed all aircraft projects undertaken from August 1914, whether

In the propeller shop, wooden two-blade propellers are being finished by hand to ensure the accuracy needed for safe and consistent operation. Final balancing was sometimes achieved by applying uneven layers of varnish. (Reproduced under licence from and courtesy of BAE SYSTEMS)

completed or not, and retrospectively allocated Type numbers in date order. The Scout C became Type 1 and the Scout D variants were covered by Types 2, 3, 4 and 5. This numbering system was then adopted for all subsequent Bristol aircraft designs.

In September 1916, the War Office contributed to the cost of a large new aircraft erecting hall. Workshops were provided to prepare the fabric and dope used for covering aeroplane wings at this time. Sir George White died in November 1916 and was succeeded by his son George 'Stanley' White as chairman of BCAC. A new canteen was built, and for the increasing number of women workers a restroom was provided. Also during 1916, the company bought Fairlawn House (built in 1874). Four years later Rodney Hall was purchased as well; this was a mid-eighteenth-century house, rebuilt in the 1890s, north of Fairlawn House. Both properties survived as part of the works until they were demolished in 1995.

During 1916 Barnwell submitted a design for an experimental two-seat reconnaissance biplane with an aluminium monocoque fuselage and metal wings – the M.R.1 (M.R. for metal reconnaissance) – and gained a contract for two evaluation aircraft. This was BCAC's first metal aircraft, later designated Type 13, which first flew in 1917 but did not go into production. It featured a tubular steel framework covered in aluminium sheet, though the steel wings continued to be covered in fabric. Making the aluminium wing spars rigid enough proved difficult and their manufacture was undertaken in Gloucester by Steel Wing Co., who had previously built experimental metal wings for other aircraft.

Barnwell began design studies for a new aircraft in March 1916, intended as an alternative to the R.E.8, the Royal Aircraft Factory successor to the B.E.2 variants. These first proposals were not pursued as Barnwell started again, to make use of the new 190 hp (142 kW) Rolls-Royce Falcon I engine. The resulting two-seat fighter and reconnaissance biplane was designated F.2A and became known as the Bristol Fighter (or popularly the 'Brisfit', subsequently allotted Type 12) and the first of two prototypes was completed in September 1916. Only fifty-two of the F.2A version were completed and the first 200 of an improved model – the F.2B (Type 14) – were assembled at Brislington (Filton again being unable to take on production), with deliveries beginning in April 1917. In the autumn of 1917, orders were received for 1,600 Bristol Fighters and by the end of the war the RAF still had over 1,500 of the type in service. Between 1916 and 1927, over 5,000 were built, including those by Standard Motors and Armstrong Whitworth, and F.2Bs served with many overseas air forces. The last F.2B in service with the RAF was withdrawn in 1932 but the type lasted a further three years with the New Zealand air force.

The works were enlarged yet again during 1917 to cope with increased orders for Bristol Fighter aircraft, both the workforce and factory doubling in size. New machine tools were installed and mass production methods were implemented to keep up with demand. During the year more than 1,000 aeroplanes were constructed, mostly F2B biplanes and M.1C (Type 20) monoplanes. Although popular with pilots, only 125 M.1Cs were built due to the War Office favouring biplanes. The following

Above: The Shuttleworth Collection's Bristol F2B Fighter was built in 1918. It was restored by the Bristol Aeroplane Company and flew again in 1952. It is seen here during an air show at Filton airfield in 1968. (M. S. 'Gill' Gillett)

Below: The Bristol M.1 monoplane was designed by Frank Barnwell as a military scout with better performance than types already serving with the RFC. This example, C4910, is one of the production M.1C series with a Le Rhône engine. (Reproduced under licence from and courtesy of BAE SYSTEMS)

year another canteen was built, an indication of a still-growing workforce. The factory had by now grown to 350,000 sq. ft (32,500 sq. m) of floor space.

Until March 1915, all aircraft purchased by the RFC had to be flown from the manufacturer to the Royal Aircraft Establishment (RAE) at Farnborough before distribution to operational squadrons to ensure standardisation and reliability. Alternatively, incomplete aeroplanes were delivered crated and assembled by the RAE and flight tested by the Aeronautical Inspection Department (AID). This potential restriction in the supply of much-needed aircraft to the front was alleviated when regional delivery centres were opened. Aircraft Acceptance Parks (AAPs), to receive aircraft from factories for flight testing and storage before distribution, a development of regional centres, were introduced in 1917 and came under the control of RFC staff who could oversee assembly and testing.

The typical AAP hangar was a triple-span general service shed with wooden Belfast roof trusses giving clear spans of 80 ft (24.4 m). The Belfast truss of a close mesh of

Radial engines, mounted on stands, are being assembled in this 1928 view inside the West Works fitting shop. All appear to be nine-cylinder Jupiter types. The Belfast truss roof timbers of the former AAP hangar can be seen. (Courtesy of Rolls-Royce Heritage Trust)

timber lattice bars set between a curved upper cord and lower tie beam dates back to the nineteenth century. The AAP at Filton was built by the Bristol Tramways & Carriage Company, for BCAC, on behalf of the Minister of War at a cost of about £5,000. The company had to buy them from the Government at the end of the war for over £80,000.

Three sets of triple sheds were erected in a row for No. 5 AAP at Filton, to the west of the Gloucester Road. Another set and an aeroplane repair section shed were erected elsewhere on the airfield and survive partly due to their being granted Grade II listed status in December 2005. This triple bay hangar became part of an operational fighter base from 1929 and, following the disbanding of No. 501 (County of Gloucester) Squadron in 1957, the hangars reverted to use by the aircraft factory. They have now been incorporated into the new Aerospace Bristol museum. Filton's AAP was used first for receiving aircraft built by BCAC, Bristol Tramways, Parnall, and Westland. The AAP closed in 1919 with the three sets of hangars surviving as part of West Works until its demolition in 1995.

Over 2,000 aircraft were constructed at Filton and Brislington in the final twelve months of the First World War, again mostly Brisfits and monoplanes. With 3,000

This view of the West Works in 1930 shows the full extent of the engine department facilities. The southern range of the hangars of the AAP was occupied by the Flying School. Across the Gloucester Road is the newly built canteen. (Courtesy of Rolls-Royce Heritage Trust)

A Bristol Type 23 Badger is part-way through construction at Filton around 1918. The mostly wooden structure can be clearly seen. It is standing in front of one of the former AAP hangars and is fitted with Palmer Cord Aero Tyres. (Reproduced under licence from and courtesy of BAE SYSTEMS)

on the payroll at the end of the war, the company looked for non-aviation work to supplement the continuing production of Bristol Fighters and to keep together its skilled workers. Contracts with the motor industry included bus and coach bodies constructed for Bristol Tramways and car bodies for Armstrong Siddeley.

The first wind tunnel at Filton was installed near Fairlawn Avenue in June 1919 to assist with testing of the Type 23 Badger development of the Fighter aeroplane. A speed of 40 mph (64 km/h) could be created within the 'open-return' tunnel, which survived until destroyed during an air raid in April 1942.

The British & Colonial Company was wound up in March 1920 and its business transferred to the Bristol Aeroplane Co. Ltd. This was done to avoid paying the government's Excess Profits Duty, which had been introduced not only to raise revenue but to reduce the profits that businesses were able to make from supplying the war effort. The new company's share capital was raised to £1 million – over half of this being secured by assets of British & Colonial.

In this 1920s view of a section of the West Works machine shop, rows of lathes built by Alfred Herbert Ltd can be seen. This company was one of the world's largest machine tool manufacturers and at one time the largest British machine tool builder. (Courtesy of Rolls-Royce Heritage Trust)

Brazil Straker and Cosmos

As Roy Fedden (1885–1973) was finishing his apprenticeship with the Bristol Motor Co. in 1906, he designed a motor car that he convinced John Brazil, of Brazil, Straker & Co., to take an interest in. Brazil Straker built London buses based on a German design at its Lodge Causeway factory in Fishponds, Bristol (built around 1906). With Fedden engaged initially as a draughtsman, the company moved into small cars, which were sold under the Straker-Squire name; Lionel Squire (c. 1868–1961) ran the London sales office. At the beginning of the First World War, the company was producing staff cars and lorries for the War Department, with Fedden then managing over 2,000 workers, including increasing numbers of women.

In 1914 the company was asked to rectify problems with Curtiss OX-5 engines, an early liquid-cooled V-8 installed in the Curtiss JN-4 'Jenny' biplane used as a trainer by RNAS pilots and flown by a few RFC squadrons. By the end of the year, Fedden and his draughtsman Leonard 'Bunny' Butler had designed significant improvements to the Curtiss engine and re-building work began at Fishponds. In January 1915, the company was brought under the Admiralty and put entirely on war work. Work on the Curtiss engines had been to such a high standard that Brazil Straker was contracted to build Rolls-Royce six-cylinder Hawk and Falcon V-12 engines under licence – the only company permitted to do so during the First World War. Nearly all Hawk engines for navy airships and the majority of Falcon engines for Bristol Fighters were built at Fishponds, along with 600 Renault 80 V-8 engines, totalling over 1,500 engines. Under the agreement, Fedden was not permitted to design his own in-line liquid-cooled engines that might compete with Rolls-Royce engines.

Fedden and Butler built the 300 hp (224 kW) Mercury in response to an Admiralty specification of 1917 for an air-cooled radial engine. Its fourteen cylinders were arranged in a helical pattern rather than two distinct rows. The second prototype Mercury was successfully tested in a Bristol Scout F aircraft and an initial order for 200 was secured, but was later cancelled. The Mercury had lost out to the inferior ABC Motors Dragonfly, which despite its shortcomings was ordered in quantity. During 1918, Fedden and Butler designed a 450 hp (331 kW) radial engine with nine

The third Bristol Scout F single-seat fighter at Filton aerodrome in 1918. This aircraft was fitted with a Cosmos Mercury radial engine instead of the Sunbeam Arab in the first two Scout Fs, which increased the top speed from 138 mph to 145 mph. (Reproduced under licence from and courtesy of BAE SYSTEMS)

The nine-cylinder single-row piston radial Jupiter became the first Bristol engine when Roy Fedden and his team moved to Filton. Engineers are making adjustments to a Jupiter with the propeller running at high speed while on test in 1921. (Courtesy of Rolls-Royce Heritage Trust)

cylinders in a single row. The Air Board ordered two prototypes of the Jupiter in July 1918 and the first was successfully bench tested in October 1918. Despite the war having ended, the Ministry of Munitions of War wrote in December asking Fedden to continue development work on the engine. In May 1919, a Jupiter engine was flight tested in one of the five Badger biplanes (achieving a speed of 142 mph – 228 km/h) and in 1919 powered a Sopwith Schneider seaplane to 165 mph (265 km/h).

By the end of 1918, Brazil Straker had been bought out by an Anglo-American financial combine with interests in mining and shipping and become Cosmos Engineering Co. At the end of 1919 the parent company failed, with reputed debts of over £1 million; the reason has been the subject of some debate, but it seems that Cosmos simply tried to expand too quickly. Nevertheless, Fedden negotiated with the official receiver to keep the design team together and carry on with work in progress. Under pressure from the Air Ministry, who had already shown faith in the Jupiter engine, the Bristol Aeroplane Company eventually purchased Cosmos to form the basis of an aero-engine department for £15,000. With Cosmos came Fedden, Butler, a team of engineers, equipment, five Jupiter engines with orders for ten more, numerous parts, and raw materials. Cosmos was wound up in February 1920 and the motor car interests sold to Straker-Squire.

Bristol Aeroplane Co.

Bristol's new engine department, formed in July 1920, was relocated to the northernmost of the former AAP sheds. The central hangar was already in use as an Experimental Flight Shed, where assembly and testing of airframes continued until at least 1925. The third, southernmost AAP hangar was used by a Reserve Flying School established by the company in 1923. By 1927 several buildings had been erected around the original sheds – a process of in-filling that continued here and across the site as the works developed.

The airframe and engine departments worked together on technical developments and the Type 32 Bullet aircraft had already been designed in 1919 specifically to test the Jupiter engine. When the Bullet appeared in July 1920, it was the first aeroplane to combine a Bristol airframe with a Bristol engine. The early 1920s were devoted mostly to development work; the Type 72 Racer of 1922 for example had several innovations, such as cantilevered monoplane with a monocoque fuselage, retractable undercarriage, and full engine cowl. Wilfred Reid designed the Racer during Frank Barnwell's absence from the company from 1921 to 1923.

The aero-engine department was not dependent on Bristol airframes to carry its products, and the worldwide sales of the Jupiter helped the company through a lean period. Income from engine sales helped develop facilities for both engine and aircraft production, with improved methods for manufacturing metal airframes. Fedden introduced high standards of engineering and new tooling and methods led

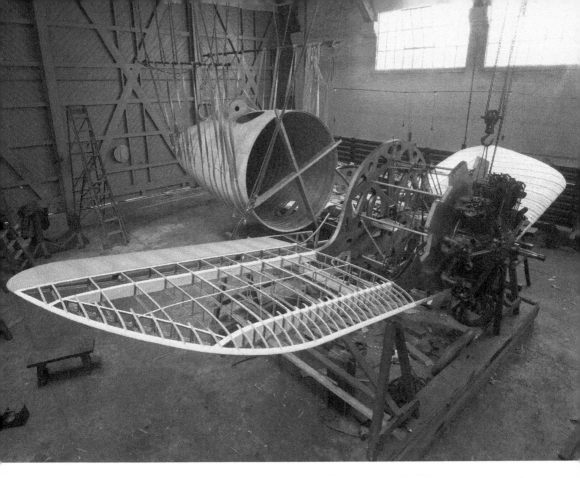

The Bristol Type 72 Racer was built as a demonstrator for the Jupiter engine and made its first flight in July 1922. The cantilevered wing, monocoque fuselage and engine mounting can be clearly seen in this view of the aircraft under construction in the experimental shed. (Reproduced under licence from and courtesy of BAE SYSTEMS)

to closer machining tolerances and improved interchangeability of parts. This was put to the test in 1923 when six Jupiters were dismantled, the parts mixed up, and the engines successfully reassembled.

There were changes too in the construction of airframes during this time. The Type 90 Berkeley biplane bomber of 1923 was the last Bristol aeroplane with the main structure formed of tubes and sockets. In the mid-1920s, chief draughtsman Tinson and Harold Pollard introduced high-tensile steel strips rolled into various sections instead of tubes. This came at a time when the Air Ministry had banned the use of wood for the main structures in RAF fighter aircraft. Pollard had joined Bristol in 1922, having previously worked for Boulton Paul Aircraft, and had become a director when he retired in 1957.

Although Bristol had several innovative designs for civil aircraft in the 1920s, it was only able to sell around fifty aircraft during the decade, not counting F2Bs and their derivatives. However, things improved when they won the competition for a

Above: The Bristol Ten-seater and Bristol Brandon were single-engine biplanes designed by Frank Barnwell with assistance from Wilfred Reid. Only three were built, two of which were used as civil transports and one of which (the Type 79 Brandon) served with the RAF. The Brandon first flew in March 1924 and could accommodate three stretchers and an attendant or two stretchers and four sitting patients. (Reproduced under licence from and courtesy of BAE SYSTEMS)

Below: In addition to service with the RAF, Bristol Bulldog biplanes were exported overseas. This view shows Bulldog serial No. 7331 (registered in May 1929), which was retained by the company as a demonstration aircraft. Seen here at Filton, test pilot Cyril Uwins is third from the right between a group of perhaps potential customers. (Reproduced under licence from and courtesy of BAE SYSTEMS)

new RAF fighter. The Type 105A Bulldog biplane was built with drawn tubes and rolled flat strips of high-tensile steel, covered with doped fabric and aluminium sheet. Nearly 450 were constructed at Filton between 1929 and 1934 at a time of little other work. After 1933, Bristol aircraft were monoplanes with a stressed skin structure made from Alclad and nearly all powered by their own engines. Alclad, a heat-treated aluminium alloy invented in America, was first used in aircraft construction in 1927. A layer of corrosion-resistant pure aluminium is bonded to a high-strength alloy core.

In 1926, Fedden and his team had already been working on an alternative to the poppet valves used on aircraft engines. In 1932 the aero-engine department produced its first radial engine with sleeve valves – the nine-cylinder Perseus. This engine powered aircraft such as the Westland Lysander army co-operation aircraft and Short C Class Empire flying boats. The engine works had extended to occupy both the centre and north AAP hangars with new buildings between and around the original structures. An imposing two-storey office block was erected facing the Gloucester Road, which was later extended with a further storey. The cast engine motifs that decorated the façade were removed and saved by the Rolls-Royce Heritage Trust when the buildings were demolished in 1995 to make way for the Royal Mail sorting office that now occupies

The headquarters building of the engine department at the former AAP that became known as West Works, in its original form as seen here in 1928. (Courtesy of Rolls-Royce Heritage Trust)

the site. In 1930 a new canteen and directors' lounge was built on the other side of the Gloucester Road. A flight operations centre was built next to the flying school by 1934, and was later extended to become Fedden House. An important development in 1935 was a new machine shop for the engine department at Patchway. This became the main aero-engine production shop; its 200,000 sq. ft (18,580 sq. m) housed over 1,000 machine tools driven by line-shafting that was powered by electric motors. It became No. 1 machine shop of the East Works. Equipment included capstan lathes, milling machines, grinders, and gas-heated case-hardening furnaces.

Rearmament and War

Bristol built its Type 142 'Britain First' prototype in response to an initiative by the owner of the *Daily Mail* newspaper, Lord Rothermere. This was a low-wing monoplane of stressed skin made from light alloy, developed from Barnwell's proposed twin-engine Type 135 that would have used the new nine-cylinder Aquila sleeve-valve radial engine. The Type 142 was powered by two of Bristol's

The private venture Bristol Type 142 Britain First aircraft was taking shape in February 1935 and is seen here under test with flaps down. The Type 142 first flew in April 1935, and tests showed that it was faster than any fighter then in service with the RAF. (Reproduced under licence from and courtesy of BAE SYSTEMS)

nine-cylinder Mercury radial engines and reached speeds of 50 mph (80 km/h) faster than the RAF's latest biplanes. In May 1935, the government determined to build up the RAF with modern equipment; soon after, Bristol Aeroplane became a public company with a share capital of £1.2 million. At this time there were 4,200 employees, the majority being in the engine works. The company was therefore well placed when the Air Ministry placed a contract for the military version of the Type 142 in September 1935. This became the Blenheim (Type 142M) light bomber, which first flew in June 1936. With this new work, the workforce expanded to over 8,000 by the end of 1935, when the factory was re-tooled and expanded for Blenheim production. The larger size and monocoque light alloy construction needed both extensions and changes in workshop practice and layout. This included doubling the floor area of the erecting halls, unchanged since 1916, a new wing assembly shop, an enlarged machine shop and tool room, new stores for the Alclad sheet, and an anodising and cadmium-plating plant.

Bristol Type 142M Blenheim light bombers in various stages of completion stand on the perimeter road at Filton. The aircraft in front appears to be taking on fuel from a portable bowser, but has no propellers. Behind the aircraft, work appears to be underway preparing the site for Rodney Works. (Reproduced under licence from and courtesy of BAE SYSTEMS)

The Britain First aircraft is the subject of the low relief sculpture on top of the tower of new Filton House, completed in April 1936. The building is now known as Pegasus House, after the sculpture seen lower down the tower façade seen in this May 1952 view from the north. (Reproduced under licence from and courtesy of BAE SYSTEMS)

A significant addition to the Filton site was the 'new' Filton House, which was built alongside the Gloucester Road next to the 'old' Filton House. The new Art-Deco-style office block was designed by Austen Hall (1881–1968) with interior mouldings and exterior sculptures in Portland stone by Denis Dunlop (1892–1959). Above the main entrance is a figure of Mercury and behind the main staircase a stained glass window designed by Jan Juta (1895–1990) features aeroplanes and Zodiac motifs. The main contractor was William Cowlin & Son Ltd, Bristol, and the building provided 88,000 sq. ft (8,175 sq. m) of office accommodation once completed in April 1936. Having stood empty and derelict for many years, the building was Grade II listed in November 1999 and restored and returned to its original use following a local campaign for its preservation. It was officially reopened in September 2013 as part of the Airbus Aerospace Park after an eighteen-month renovation programme.

The nine-cylinder Pegasus radial engine was almost identical in size and construction to the earlier Jupiter, but various improvements increased engine speed and power to 815 hp (608 kW) in late versions. A supercharged Pegasus was used in the Type 138A High Altitude Monoplane that set two world flight altitude records in September 1936 and June 1937, the second being at 53,937 ft (16,440 m).

A section of an East Works machine shop in November 1936. The universal grinders in the foreground have independent electrically powered motors, while others still have overhead belts driven by common motors. (Courtesy of Rolls-Royce Heritage Trust)

A new wind tunnel was constructed next to the existing one in 1936. Wind speeds of 95 mph (152 km/h) were produced. The first aircraft models tested were of the Blenheim and the last one for Concorde, before the tunnel was abandoned in 1969. There were further developments for the engine department in 1936 too; a two-storey office block was built on the east side of the Gloucester Road (in front of the new machine shop) and survived in use until the East Works site was vacated by Rolls-Royce. Further south on the opposite side of the road, Rodney Works was erected to specialise in engine cowlings and exhaust systems. This continued in use until 1991 and was demolished in December 1995.

Early in 1936 it became clear that the UK aircraft industry could not meet the government's schemes to expand the RAF in response to re-armament in Germany. A programme of building shadow factories, firstly beside car works, was established by the Air Ministry and in 1937 a new assembly and test facility was completed at Patchway's East Works. By the end of the year the first shadow-built Bristol Mercury engine was tested.

A further three large workshops were erected on the East Works site between 1936 and 1939 and these were linked to the West Works by a tunnel under the Gloucester

A nine-cylinder radial engine, probably a Mercury, is in a Shadow Factory test bed in December 1938. The indicator dials gave engine oil temperature and pressure, fuel pressure, and air speed readings. (Courtesy of Rolls-Royce Heritage Trust)

Road. A fleet of small trucks were used to transport engines and components between the two sites. Numerous engine test beds and a foundry completed the facilities on the East Works by the start of the Second World War.

The Type 156 Beaufighter twin-engine heavy fighter aircraft of 1939 was developed from the fourteen-cylinder Taurus-powered Type 152 Beaufort torpedo bomber, itself derived from the Blenheim. The Beaufighter used the fourteen-cylinder, two-row sleeve valve Hercules engine. First run in 1936, more Hercules engines were built than any other Bristol type. Power had been increased from 1,150 hp (857 kW) to 1,725 hp (1,286 kW) by 1943. Bristol Siddeley Engines were listing the Hercules as a current model in 1962, by which time 70,000 were claimed to have been built. The Ministry of Aircraft Production established shadow factories at Oldmixon and Banwell (not to be confused with Barnwell) in north Somerset in 1941. Bristol used these to build and repair Beaufort, Beaufighter, and Hawker Tempest aircraft. Most

The Bristol Type 156 Beaufighter was a multirole aircraft that first flew in July 1939 and entered service with the RAF a year later. This image is of a mock-up of the aircraft recorded in March 1939. (Reproduced under licence from and courtesy of BAE SYSTEMS)

of the Beaufighters (3,336 in total) were assembled at Oldmixon from parts made at Bridgwater, Banwell, and Filton.

When war was declared in September 1939, the Bristol company had the largest single aviation manufacturing unit in the world, with over 2,500,000 sq. ft (232,257 sq. m) of covered floor space. During the war, more than 14,000 aircraft and 101,000 engines were built directly or by shadow manufacturers. In 1942 the company reached its peak employment of 52,000 personnel, with the population of the surrounding communities having also grown by the start of the war. There had been major development in what became Patchway at the end of the 1930s, and Filton's population grew from around 3,000 in 1931 to 10,000 by 1939.

Wartime expansion of the engine department led to development of more land at Patchway, north of Gipsy Patch Lane, including more engine test beds. This site continues to serve aero-engine manufacture by Rolls-Royce. Both Filton and Patchway sites continued to develop after the war and a new drawing office was built on the site of the destroyed wind tunnel. Company architect Eric Ross designed the distinctive building in a contemporary style, with pointed irregular stone walling, glazed frontage, and full-width steps to the entrance.

Women were once again recruited to replace men called to active service during the Second World War and undertook a wide range of engineering and machining tasks, including welding and operating machine tools as seen in Rodney Works in January 1942. (Reproduced under licence from and courtesy of BAE SYSTEMS)

The new aircraft design drawing office provided at the end of the Second World War was designed by company architect Eric Ross in a contemporary style. The Rover 14 car beside it looks positively old-fashioned. (Reproduced under licence from and courtesy of BAE SYSTEMS)

Towards the end of the Second World War, the company began to consider civil aviation opportunities. Recommendations by the Brabazon Committee, formed in December 1942, had included proposals for an express Atlantic airliner. Bristol was awarded the contract for the Brabazon airliner as other firms involved in production of large aircraft had no capacity at the time. Two prototypes of an airliner with a high standard of comfort and high capacity were required. When the dimensions for the Type 167 Brabazon had been established, it was clear that a new aircraft assembly hall (AAH) would be required for its construction. The building, designed by Ross with David Aberdeen, was to become the largest of its kind in the world, with a floor area of 7.5 acres (3 hectares). Construction of the AAH began, in October 1945, but it was not fully finished for nearly four years; causes of delays included bad weather in 1947 and an embargo on the transport of steel. The first Brabazon prototype therefore began in October 1945 in an existing flight shed and the incomplete aircraft was towed to the east bay of the AAH two years later.

Not only did the Brabazon airliner need a new building for its construction, but an extension of the airfield runway to 8,250 ft (2,515 m) was also required, which resulted in the destruction of Charlton village. The first prototype flew in September 1949, but in July 1953 the Government cancelled the project due to a lack of civil or military orders as the aircraft was at that time perceived as being too big. The 177-ft-long (54-m) fuselage had skin-plating carried on Z-section stringers and rolled,

Construction of the first prototype Bristol Type 167 Brabazon airliner was started in 1945 in one of the existing sheds while the AAH was still being built. The incomplete fuselage and wing sections were moved to the AAH in October 1947. (Reproduced under licence from and courtesy of BAE SYSTEMS)

channel-section frames. It was at the time one of the largest aircraft ever built, and ahead of its time in that respect – perhaps demonstrated by the current double-deck Airbus A380 airliner with its overall length of 238 ft. (72.5 m). The then needs of the civil aircraft industry had already moved on, as seen in the de Havilland Comet jet airliner. Both prototypes were cut up in October 1953, the second one not being completed, and only a few relics remain of this iconic aircraft.

Alongside the Brabazon project, the Type 170 Freighter transport plane was being developed. Powered by two of the company's own Hercules 734 engines, over 200 of this and the Wayfarer passenger variant were built between 1945 and 1958. For the passenger version the nose doors were omitted and additional windows were added; the Mk IIA Wayfarer had thirty-two seats. Although sleeve-valve radial-engine design and production continued, efforts were made to enter the jet age from 1941, and the first Bristol gas turbine engine was the Theseus in 1947.

An Austin 10 car is posed on the ramp into a Bristol Type 170 Freighter, perhaps best known for their use as an air car-ferry. The fuselage of a Mk IIA Wayfarer passenger version can be seen in the background. (Reproduced under licence from and courtesy of BAE SYSTEMS)

Diversification

After the war, Bristol made efforts to minimise the effects of transition to peacetime through diversification. The Armaments Division, set up in 1935 to develop power-operated aircraft gun turrets, was split into the Plastics Division and the Car Division. The Plastics Division used the wartime experience of moulding cockpit glazing, gun turrets, and radar domes from plastics such as Perspex. Post-war the Division worked with a variety of composite materials including fibre-glass and Durestos (a felt-like moulding material made of asbestos fibres and synthetic resin) to produce items such as aircraft drop tanks. Between 1954 and 1985 over 20,000 fuel tanks of 100- to 300-gallon (454- to 1,363-litre) capacity were produced for all front-line RAF fighters. In 1958 the Division became a separate company – Bristol Aeroplane Plastics Ltd manufacturing fuel tanks, car bodywork, water pipes, gun turrets and sailing dinghies. In 1968 this company was purchased by Rolls-Royce, which was wanting a readymade production facility for composite materials. A new

The post-war Plastics Division produced drop fuel tanks for aircraft made from Durestos, an asbestos-based composite. These two drop tanks are destined for an English Electric Canberra jet bomber. (Reproduced under licence from and courtesy of BAE SYSTEMS)

factory with 200,000 sq. ft (18,580 sq. m) of manufacturing space was established in Shirehampton, Bristol, in 1969. All plastic-related facilities at Filton were transferred the following year.

The Car Division, which produced hand-built, high-performance cars constructed to aircraft standards, passed into private ownership in 1960 as Bristol Cars. For a time from 1951, car manufacture took place in the former Shield's Laundry (reconstructed in 1923) opposite Filton House, which was purchased by Bristol Aeroplane. The Laundry was sold to Bristol Siddeley in July 1960, passing to use for education in 1965 until finally being demolished in 1998.

Another diversification was the manufacture of prefabricated houses and other buildings using aluminium left over from war-time aircraft construction. This continued until 1955 when more conventional building materials became readily available again. The term 'prefab' was used by the Minister of Works, Lord Portal, when preparing a scheme for single-storey steel houses in 1944. The Minister of Aircraft Production decided that aircraft manufacturers were an obvious choice for their construction, and a shortage of steel led to the use of aluminium. Later, in 1944, a small design team called the Aircraft Industries Research Organisation for Housing (AIROH) was set up.

Bristol Aeroplane decided that it would focus housing production at Weston-super-Mare, with Oldmixon as the lead of five factory sites. The change-over from aircraft production was reputedly so rapid and efficient that the first prefabs were being erected at the start of the assembly line as the last aircraft reached the other end. The first Bristol-built AIROH prefab was erected in Shirehampton, Bristol, in September 1946. In less than three years the Weston works had produced 11,250 prefabs for distribution throughout the south of England. In anticipation of a decline in demand for prefab houses, the company began producing schools, hospitals, and other buildings. Their first aluminium school was erected in Lockleaze, Bristol, in 1948. Over 400 prefabricated school buildings were in use in the UK by 1954, with many units also being sold overseas. Bristol Aeroplane's apprentice school of 1954 was built mainly by use of their own multi-storey system.

In 1954 the company opened a technical college for apprentices and trainees opposite Rodney Works. The building made extensive use of the company's own prefabricated multi-storey system. This was eventually absorbed by Filton Technical College, which had opened nearby in 1961. (Reproduced under licence from and courtesy of BAE SYSTEMS)

Bristol established a Helicopter Division at Filton in 1944 to develop the designs of division head Raoul Hafner (1905–1980), who had come to Britain in 1933 after experimenting with helicopters in Austria. The single-rotor Type 171 Sycamore was the result, which first flew in July 1947 and was the first British helicopter to receive a certificate of airworthiness. It was supplied to military and civil operators and 180 had been built by 1959. New test facilities were provided to simulate flight conditions, and a gantry to suspend a complete helicopter by its rotor hub was built. A rotor test tower was erected west of the assembly shops in 1945; a screen of heavy steel netting surrounded the top to provide protection in the event of a rotor blade failure. The Type 171 rotor was endurance-tested for seventy hours in this tower. A much larger gantry, like a Bailey Bridge, was built with clearance for both rotors of the later Type 173 tandem helicopter of 1952, which combined two sets of Sycamore power plant.

The Brabazon Committee had also recommended a medium-range transport aircraft for 'Empire' services, which in time became the Type 175 Britannia. The

The Type 171 helicopter was named after seeds of the sycamore tree. Here, a Sycamore model is mounted for wind tunnel testing in August 1945. (Reproduced under licence from and courtesy of BAE SYSTEMS)

Ministry of Supply (MoS) ordered three prototypes from Bristol in July 1948, each to be powered by four of their eighteen-cylinder, two-row sleeve valve Centaurus piston engines, but with two able to be converted to the Proteus free turbine engine then being developed. Only two prototypes were in fact built, and both with Proteus 'jet' engines – the first being flown in August 1952 at the hands of chief test pilot A. J. 'Bill' Pegg (1906–1978). Final assembly of Britannia aircraft took place in the former Brabazon assembly hall, aided by the use of overhead cranes and wheeled cradle carriages. By 1960, when they had been superseded by the de Havilland Comet 4 and Boeing 707 turbojets, a total of eighty-five examples of the Britannia and its variants had been built at Filton and by Short Bros. & Harland in Belfast. This was not quite the end for the Britannia though, as the type was further developed under licence by Canadair Ltd in Montreal in the 1960s.

Bristol had begun the manufacture of motor cases for missiles and research rockets shortly after the war. By the early 1950s, the expanding rocket motor business at Filton was outgrowing its accommodation in Rodney Works and it was decided to relocate this to the former shadow factory at Oldmixon. Pits were accordingly excavated in 1953 for heat-treatment furnaces and quench tanks. However, the move to Oldmixon of the Helicopter Division in 1955 and increased rocket motor activity prompted a further move. The rundown of AIROH manufacturing meant that the Banwell factory was underused and rocket motor manufacturing moved once again

The prototype Bristol Type 175 Britannia airliner stands on the apron outside the AAH in July 1952. This aircraft was retained by the company for flight development and engine testing, including tropical performance trials, and for conversion flying for BOAC pilots. (Reproduced under licence from and courtesy of BAE SYSTEMS)

The aircraft factory at Filton in 1952, looking north-west across the Gloucester Road. Facing the road are both 'old' and 'new' Filton Houses, with the much-enlarged 1910 sheds immediately behind and to the left of Fairlawn Avenue. Beyond are two former canteens and the drawing office. The large rectangular building behind these is the 1220 laboratory. The AAH is at the far side of the site. The former Shields Laundry, used by the Car Division, is in the foreground. (Reproduced under licence from and courtesy of BAE SYSTEMS)

in 1956. The British Messier rocket motor team at Rotol, Gloucestershire, also relocated to Banwell.

Once the required facilities had been installed at Banwell, production resumed of rocket motors and high-pressure gas storage bottles for aircraft and missiles. Booster, sustainer and third-stage rocket motors for the Skylark rocket were produced from 1956. Meanwhile, discussions had been started with the American missile business Aerojet General, with the hope of Bristol acquiring its own propellant manufacturing capacity, without having to resort to the Royal Ordnance Factory (ROF). In December 1959, Bristol Aerojet (BAJ) was incorporated as a joint venture with Aerojet General.

By the early 1960s BAJ was producing 6,000 rocket motor tubes a year, including cases for the Sea Cat, Sea Slug, and later Rapier missile systems. The company also secured a contract to provide Gosling boost motors for the Bloodhound and Thunderbird guided weapons. The technical partnership with Aerojet General ended in 1970, with no propellant deal. BAJ developed the apogee stage motor to place the telecom satellite Prospero in orbit in 1971. But BAJ had financial problems due to an

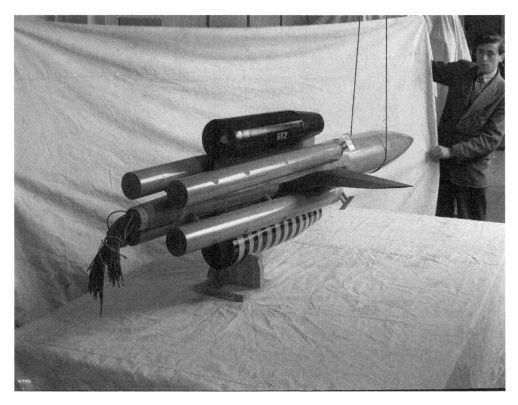

A Bristol Bloodhound model is prepared for wind tunnel testing in April 1953, complete with representations of ramjets and booster rockets. (Reproduced under licence from and courtesy of BAE SYSTEMS)

unsuccessful attempt to diversify and the failure of major shareholder Rolls-Royce. The liquidation of Rolls-Royce led to BAJ being acquired by Vickers Engineering in 1979. Rationalisation and restructuring of Vickers in 1984 resulted in a management buy-out of BAJ, but with reduction in demand for defence-related products, BAJ was sold to Meggitt Holdings in 1987. By 1991 it was not possible to sustain the rocket motor business, which was sold to the ROF. The Bristol Aero Collection occupied one of the Banwell shops from 1993 to 1996, before moving to Kemble airfield. The works were later demolished to make way for a housing development.

Bristol Bloodhound

After the Second World War, the UK's air defences had been run down in the belief that another conflict would be unlikely for some time. This policy was revised in the light of the USSR developing its nuclear capability from 1949. An integrated network of radar and interceptor aircraft with ground missiles as a final line of defence was then proposed. All three military services had identified a requirement for surface-to-air-guided-weapons (SAGW) with ranges of 15 to 150 miles (24 to 240 km); those for the Royal Navy and Army were prioritised by the government. Bristol was approached by the MoS to develop a back-up to contracts issued to Armstrong Whitworth Aircraft and the English Electric Company. Though Bristol could build the airframe and propulsion systems, the company had no experience of developing electronic guidance systems and Ferranti Ltd, near Manchester, was brought onboard.

A team of engineers from Bristol and Ferranti had been sent secretly to the RAE Farnborough and other government research establishments in mid-1949 to learn about the latest developments in guided missiles and the radar systems required to control them. On their return to Filton, a Guided Weapons Department was established as part of the Armaments Division; a separate Guided Weapons Division was later formed. Following these visits Bristol proposed a ramjet propulsion system to give the missile long range, and Ferranti proposed a guidance system using semi-active radar homing. The MoS accepted these proposals and Bristol was given a contract that covered the overall design of the missile airframe and launcher, with the design and development of the ramjet sub-contracted to the Engine Division at Patchway. Ferranti was awarded a separate contract for electronics in the missile and the fire control system.

There being no supersonic wind tunnel available, early design work was done with free flight models at Larkhill range. Ramjet development at Larkhill used a small Jet Test Vehicle, which was fired during 1950 and 1951. A full-scale development contract was signed in April 1951, by which time the missile had been allocated the codename 'Red Duster'. Most of the development missiles and test vehicles were built at Filton and the prototype missile first flew in November 1955. Meanwhile, the government decided that the RAF would take control of surface-to-air-missile defence in the UK, and the Red Duster was adopted as an interim stage system with which the RAF could gain knowledge in the operation and maintenance of an SAGW, ahead of a follow-up system that would fully meet its operational requirements.

Bristol was awarded a contract to supply 800 Red Duster missiles in late 1955, which was officially named the Bristol-Ferranti Bloodhound in 1956. Production of the Bloodhound missile main body, fins and radome (which housed the homing head dish) was undertaken at the Bristol Aircraft factory in Cardiff. The Bloodhound Mk I had a range of 32 miles (52 km) and a maximum speed of Mach 2.2. Propulsion was provided by four BAJ Gosling booster rockets that launched the missile; these fell away when thrust from the two Thor ramjets exceeded that of the boosters. The Gosling motor cases were filled with propellant by the ROF. Provision of the warhead was also undertaken by the ROF. Dowty of Cheltenham provided some of the hydraulic components.

Sales of Bloodhound overseas generated much-needed income for the company at a difficult time. The system was ordered by Sweden in small numbers for trials and training during 1959. The Royal Australian Air Force (RAAF) system entered service in January 1961 and lasted until 1968. The R&D contract was signed off in October

The 1220 Project laboratory was constructed in connection with development of the Bristol Bloodhound guided missile. It is seen here shortly after completion in April 1952. This part of the site is now occupied by Airbus's Barnwell House. (Reproduced under licence from and courtesy of BAE SYSTEMS)

Above: The ramjet development facility at Patchway was alongside the railway line at the extreme eastern edge of the Gipsy Patch Lane site, as seen here in October 1953. The two buildings to the left each contained a pair of full-scale ramjet test beds. (Courtesy of Rolls-Royce Heritage Trust)

Below: Staff are enjoying a break in the May sunshine at the rear of the new canteen in 1952. The canteen was located to the south-west of the aircraft factory across Golf Course Lane. (Reproduced under licence from and courtesy of BAE SYSTEMS)

1961, though post design services carried on until the end of service with the RAF in 1964 and longer for the RAAF.

Development of the follow-on system started in late 1955, with the missile given the codename 'Blue Envoy', but intelligence gathered on Soviet military intentions rendered the system redundant and the Stage Plan was abandoned as part of the '1957 White Paper on Defence'. The Bristol and Ferranti engineers, aware of the possible demise of Blue Envoy before it happened, proposed several advanced versions of Bloodhound to the MoS. Proposals for a conventional missile and one with a nuclear warhead were approved for initial development in 1958. Originally planned for air defence of the UK, their role was changed in 1960, and the conventional Bloodhound Mk II only was approved for development as a transportable system for defence of RAF bases in the Middle and Far East. Production followed much the same pattern as the Mk I, though the building of the launcher may have involved Filton. Ferranti developed a rader guidance technique for the Mk I that overcame major limitations in the system used on the Mk I. The Mk I missile's maximum speed was Mach 2.55 and its range was increased to up to 100 miles (160 km) by using more powerful Gosling XV boost motors, the redesigned Thor 200 Series ramjet, extra fuel capacity, and a trajectory control system that allowed the missile to spend most of its flight at high altitude.

Production missile deliveries to the RAF started in December 1963 and the first squadron reached initial operational capability in November 1965. The only major upgrade was to the computer and display systems in 1986 to 1988, some of which involved the by then BAe Naval Weapons Division at Filton. Three other nations used Bloodhound Mk II: Sweden (1964 until the late 1970s); Switzerland (1964 to 1999); and Singapore (1970 to 1990). The RAF Bloodhound force was rapidly run down after the fall of the Berlin Wall, and in July 1991 the system was retired from service in the UK. Post design services for Bloodhound were moved from Filton to Stevenage for the remainder of the system's service with Switzerland.

More Development

A third wind tunnel, designed by the Guided Weapons Department in late 1950, was completed in June 1952. It was the largest privately owned supersonic tunnel at the time and used high-pressure air from Proteus compressors to achieve speeds of Mach 3 (i.e. up to three times the speed of sound). Only models of the Bloodhound missile and Type 188 aircraft were tested before the tunnel was abandoned in 1956. Parts of the tunnel still existed within the Rolls-Royce Gipsy Patch Lane site until at least 1995. The High Altitude Test Plant (HATP) was developed during 1956 and 1957 to simulate the conditions of high-speed flight at high altitudes in the development of ramjets. Built to the north of the Gipsy Patch Lane site, the HATP could create conditions equivalent to speeds of more than Mach 3 at altitudes up to 90,000 ft (27,432 m).

This view looking west, from October 1959, shows most of the Bristol Siddeley site. To the south of Gipsy Patch Lane are the 1930s factories and engine test beds of East Works, and beyond them the smaller West Works site. On the Gipsy Patch Lane site, the High Altitude Test Plant is to the extreme right and engine test beds are in the middle. (Courtesy of Rolls-Royce Heritage Trust)

The light alloys that began to be used in airframe construction from the 1930s were more prone to fatigue damage than the wood and steel used before. During the Second World War aircraft life was tragically short and manufacturers did not have the resources to deal with what was at the time an academic problem. At the end of the war, with the construction of civil aircraft, more attention was paid to the effects of component fatigue. A laboratory was established in 1948 and was enlarged twice in the 1950s for additional test machinery. After the de Havilland Comet disaster of 1954, it was decided that full-scale tests of fuselage components and complete airframes were necessary, and facilities were duly provided at Filton.

The third wind tunnel at Filton, and the fourth overall, was commissioned in 1956 when the company's future was thought to lie in large transport aircraft, and there were concerns about the 'scale effects' of testing from models that were too small. This tunnel was of closed return design, with a closed test section; the circuit was constructed from wood with steel corners and supports. Much work was carried out testing for the SST (supersonic transport) and subsequent Concorde projects.

This view from May 1955 of the fourth wind tunnel at Filton under construction shows the steel framework for the closed-circuit tunnel and the contemporary building design. (Reproduced under licence from and courtesy of BAE SYSTEMS)

The tunnel was built with a test section that was 12 ft (3.6 m) wide, 10 ft (3 m) high, and 25 ft (7.6 m) long. One 850 hp (634 kW) AC and two 55 hp (41 kW) DC motors driving the 22 ft diameter (6.7 m) fan produced a maximum speed of 195 mph (312 km/h). By 1989 the wind tunnel had been re-motored and refurbished. Weather protection was provided by external cladding and a new machine shop was added to the north side.

The aero-engine side of the business continued to develop in the 1950s, with further test facilities at both the East Works and Gypsy Patch Lane sites. The Orpheus, developed by Stanley Hooker (1907–1984), was claimed to be the most advanced medium-thrust lightweight turbojet of its day. The Orpheus was the power plant for the Folland Gnat lightweight fighter, which first flew in July 1955 and became well known through its use by the RAF Red Arrows aerobatic team. The Olympus turbojet of 1952 pioneered the twin-spool principle, and became the power plant for the Avro (later Hawker Siddeley) Vulcan nuclear V-bomber that was introduced in 1956 (first flight 1952) and the British Aircraft Corporation's TSR-2 tactical strike and reconnaissance aircraft, which first flew in September 1964 but was subsequently cancelled by the government due to rising costs. A more powerful

This image from around 1959 shows Orpheus-turbojet-powered Folland Gnats of the Finnish Air Force. (Courtesy of Rolls-Royce Heritage Trust)

Olympus turbojet engines being assembled by Bristol Siddeley at Patchway in around 1959; the engines are on platforms that can be raised or lowered. The Olympus was developed by Bristol Aero Engines from 1946 and was the power plant for the Avro Vulcan V-bomber. (Courtesy of Rolls-Royce Heritage Trust)

version – the Olympus 593 – was developed with Snecma of France in the early 1960s for the Concorde supersonic airliner.

In March 1953, a site to the south of the East Works engine test beds, next to the test rig for the Brabazon's coupled Centaurus engines, was cleared for a new test house designed by Ross. This could accommodate engines up to 6,000 hp (4,474 kW), including the Proteus turbojet, and was completed in April 1954. The building combined a pair of soundproof test cells with air intake and exhaust silencing baffles either side of a central control room. It was later used as a display area by the Bristol branch of the Rolls-Royce Heritage Trust but was demolished by 2007.

The development of the more powerful Olympus turbojets led to the construction in 1957 of test beds able to take engines of 40,000 lbs (18,143 kg) thrust. These

Further pairs of test beds for development of the Olympus jet engine were built on the Gipsy Patch Lane site. The nearer pair here was built around 1957 and those behind date from 1950. The open water tank in front of the intake helped to ensure that the air drawn in was free of grit. (Courtesy of Rolls-Royce Heritage Trust)

were like the earlier Proteus test beds, with twin cells either side of a central control room. Exhaust silencing (a relative term!) was achieved by twin detuners, discharging upwards at their downstream end. These buildings remain on the Gipsy Patch, but computer control and digital recording had replaced the original gauges, pen plotters, and clipboards by the 1990s, and the staffing required to oversee engine tests was reduced from over a dozen to just two or three people.

Bristol Siddeley and the British Aircraft Corporation

Bristol Aeroplane divided its major operations in 1956 into Bristol Aircraft and Bristol Aero Engines. In April 1959, under government pressure to reduce the number of aerospace manufacturers, Bristol Aero Engines and Armstrong Siddeley Motors merged to form Bristol Siddeley Engines Ltd, with Bristol holding a 50 per cent share.

The engine department headquarters with added third storey, as seen in May 1952. A Bristol 401 car is in pole position by the entrance, while lesser Vauxhall and Standard models are in the car park. (Courtesy of Rolls-Royce Heritage Trust)

In 1961 Bristol Siddeley (BS) was expanded by the purchase of the de Havilland Engine Company and the engine division of Blackburn Aircraft.

There had been strong indications from the government that it also expected consolidation within the aircraft manufacturers. Incentives for such a merger included the TSR-2 aircraft contract. In a parallel move to the creation of BS, the aircraft business of Bristol Aeroplane was merged in 1960 with English Electric Aviation Ltd and Vickers-Armstrongs (Aviation) to form the British Aircraft Corporation (BAC), which subsequently also acquired a 70 per cent share of Hunting Aircraft. Bristol continued to have holdings outside BAC, owning half of BAJ and a 10 per cent share of helicopter manufacturer Westland Aircraft. The Corporation was split into two divisions – Aircraft and Guided Weapons. The parent companies became subsidiaries of BAC, with Filton's airframe side trading as Bristol Aircraft Ltd.

Bristol's still separate Guided Weapons Division was acquired by BAC in 1963, along with that of English Electric, to form a new subsidiary BAC (Guided Weapons). Filton was involved in the development of the Swingfire anti-tank missile (used from 1966); Rapier surface-to-air missile (introduced 1971); Sea Wolf shipborne-guided surface-to-air missile (1979); and Sea Skua helicopter-launched naval air-to-surface missile (1982). The Division later included electronics and space systems.

A Harrier GR3 'jump jet' hovers in front of the glazed north wall of the AAH during an airfield display in June 1968. The success of the Harrier is largely due to the Pegasus turbofan, which provides both lift and forward propulsion. (M. S. 'Gill' Gillett)

The Pegasus vectored-thrust turbofan engine was developed by BS from 1956 for the Hawker P.1127 and the Hawker Siddeley Kestrel experimental V/STOL (vertical/short take-off and landing) aircraft, which were first flown in 1960 and 1964 respectively. This led to the highly successful Hawker Siddeley Harrier 'jump jet', which was first flown in December 1967 and remained in service with the RAF from 1969 until 2006. The later Sea Harrier was also retired from Royal Navy service in 2006. It was the first successful V/STOL fighter-bomber.

By 1961 BS was managing sites in the region at Patchway (research, bench, and flight development, design, sales & commercial offices, and apprentice school); Rodney Works (sheet metal components for installations and power plants); Whitchurch Aerodrome, north Somerset (two hangars used for engine repairs and overhaul); and Bentham, Gloucestershire (sheet metal and other components; engine repair and overhaul). Bristol Siddeley later took over part of the Gloster Aircraft factory at Brockworth for production of Armstrong Siddeley Sapphire turbojet engines. The Patchway site continued to develop in the 1960s, including further engine test facilities. A new headquarters office was built during 1962 to 1964 and named Whittle House in honour of the British jet engine pioneer Frank Whittle. Rolls-Royce purchased BS in 1966 to become the only major UK aero engine manufacturer. In 1971 financial problems, mainly caused by problems with development of the RB211 turbofan engine at Derby, led to Rolls-Royce going into liquidation and the aero

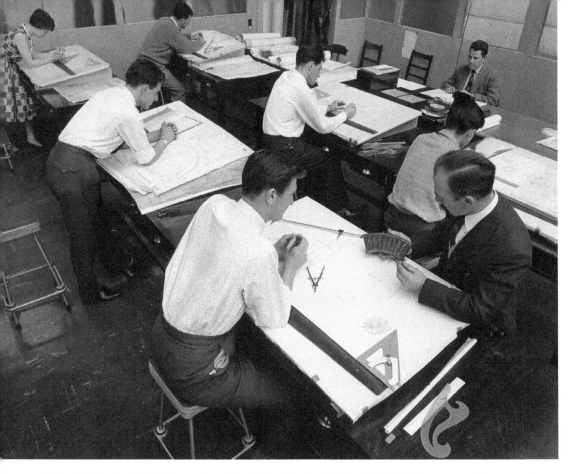

Slide rules, not calculators, are the order of the day in the Bristol Siddeley drawing office, around 1959, together with set squares, compasses, French curves and drawing boards. (Courtesy of Rolls-Royce Heritage Trust)

engine business was nationalised; its remaining interests in BAC were sold to Vickers and GEC. The government re-privatised Rolls-Royce by selling-off its shares in 1987.

The first Bristol turbojet aeroplane was the Type 188, developed from 1953, which was produced for research into supersonic flight. The first of the fully equipped prototype aircraft flew in April 1962 at the hands of Bristol's chief test pilot Godfrey Auty (1921–2001). A third airframe was sent by road to the RAE at Farnborough in 1960 for structural tests. The aircraft were constructed in stainless steel to withstand the kinetic heating effects of supersonic flight, for which a new argon arc-welding technique was developed. However, the excessive fuel consumption of the two de Havilland Gyron Junior engines did not allow the aircraft to fly at high speeds for long enough to evaluate the thermal soaking of the airframe as intended, and the programme was abandoned in 1964. The Type 188 and Type 221 were the last 'Bristol' designs to reach prototype stage. The Type 221 had started out as one of two Fairey Delta 2 supersonic research aircraft, which was rebuilt in 1964 with a slender ogee-shaped wing instead of the original delta. By 1964 some 15,750 aircraft

Above: The Bristol Type 188 jet aircraft, built as part of the supersonic flight research programme, was nicknamed the *Flaming Pencil*. (Reproduced under licence from and courtesy of BAE SYSTEMS)

Below: The Bristol Type 221 aircraft was constructed as an experimental jet to test wing shapes, in connection with the Concorde supersonic airliner programme, and was used from 1964 until 1973. (Reproduced under licence from and courtesy of BAE SYSTEMS)

of eighty different designs had been built in Bristol's own works and its directly managed shadow factories.

Following a lull in airframe production in the late 1950s, work began on the Concorde supersonic transport aircraft in 1962. The project was allocated to Bristol partially because the end of Britannia production left a shortage of work, but the large assembly hall and long runway created for the Brabazon were additional factors. Filton was established as the final British assembly base for Concorde, with fuselage and wing assemblies coming from Toulouse, France, and Weybridge, Surrey. Construction was almost entirely from aluminium alloys and, early in 1964, 700 lb (318 kg) blocks were reduced to airframe sections a tenth of their original size by electro etching and computer-managed cutting machines. Final assembly of the British prototype Concorde 002 began in August 1968 and its first flight was on 9 April 1969, just over a month after that of the French prototype 001 on 2 March.

Employment in the Bristol-based companies reached 30,000 in the late 1960s, but the end of the post war boom was signalled by 700 workers at Rolls-Royce being laid off in 1968. This was despite the approaching first flights for Concorde. The

The Filton-built British Concorde prototype 002 takes off from Fairford airfield on its first supersonic flight on 25 March 1970. Concorde 002 has been preserved at the Fleet Air Arm Museum at Yeovilton, Somerset, since 1976. (Reproduced under licence from and courtesy of BAE SYSTEMS)

Pre-production Concorde 101, nearing completion in the AAH at Filton, from where it made its first flight on 17 December 1971, was used to develop the final design of the production aircraft. It made its final flight in 1977 to the Imperial War Museum Duxford. (Reproduced under licence from and courtesy of BAE SYSTEMS)

following year the Bristol Siddeley Engines combined stewards' committee had pushed for workers' control of the industry. By the mid-1970s, trade unions in the aircraft industry were making links between the case for social ownership and ensuring that the Concorde project continued. Official union policy, however, was for nationalisation, which was achieved in 1977 by the Aircraft and Shipbuilding Industries Act following election of the Labour Government in 1974 to create British Aerospace.

The early 1970s was a period of discontent and disruption in Bristol's aircraft industry. Over 3,000 manual workers held a series of token stoppages in support of a pay rise in April 1970. The following year redundancy and pay disputes led to walkouts involving over 6,000 workers; at Rolls-Royce, they lasted nine weeks. In 1974 a ten-day strike by aircraft clerical workers caused the loss of 15,600 working days. The trade unions' use of 'guerrilla'-type tactics, such as locking management out of new Filton House, drew scorn from some sections of the national press, but this did not prevent managers helping the unions to prepare the case for not cancelling Concorde, which was presented to the Government by a large delegation at Downing Street.

Space

The 'Space Race' was in full swing in the 1960s when BAC made its entry into this new technology at Filton, building on earlier work on rocket motors and guided weapons. The Skylark had been the UK's first rocket to reach space when its fourth development launch by the RAE in 1957 marked the beginning of Britain's space science programme. By the end of its forty-eight-year programme, 441 Skylarks had been fired from Woomera in Australia and other launch sites around the world. Skylarks carried many diverse scientific instruments and technology payloads into the upper atmosphere and near space.

BAC became the prime contractor for the Skylark programme in 1964 and in 1967 transferred all space work to the newly formed Space & Instrumentations Group, within the Space & Guided Weapons Division at Filton. The earliest Skylark rockets were powered by a single-stage Raven motor produced by BAJ. The first two-stage

An RCS (reaction control system) satellite subsystem is being prepared for a spin or leak test in this view from 1965. This RCS has four conical propellant tanks, and was probably part of the Intelsat programme. (Reproduced under licence from and courtesy of BAE SYSTEMS)

launch was in April 1960 with a Cuckoo booster rocket. The first Skylark prepared at Filton was launched in June 1968, by which date a new booster rocket – the Goldfinch – had been introduced. There were continuing improvements in the rocket motors and by 1976 the Type 12 Skylark was powered with a Goldfinch II booster, Raven XI sustainer (main motor), and a third-stage Cuckoo II or IV engine. BAC also marketed the smaller Skua and Petrel sounding rockets produced by BAJ.

The International Telecommunications Satellite Organisation's first satellite was built by Hughes Aircraft and launched in the USA in April 1965. Later, in the 1960s, BAC was appointed as sub-contractors to Hughes and Intelsat IV F-4 was assembled and tested at Filton using parts produced in Europe, before being launched in January 1972. Prospero was the one and only UK satellite launched by a UK vehicle (the Black Arrow rocket), with Bristol making and testing structures and being involved in the launch campaign at Woomera in 1971. It studied the effects of the space environment on communications satellites.

Ariel was a UK satellite research programme conducted by the SRC (Science Research Council). Ariel 1, launched in April 1962, and Ariel 2 were built in the USA on behalf of the SRC. Ariel 3 was the first satellite designed and constructed in the UK, albeit as a subcontractor to an American company. When BAe was appointed prime contractor for Ariel 4, it was the first time a UK company had taken this role for a satellite. It was launched in December 1971 and recorded characteristics of low energy changes through detecting radio noise. The final of the series, Ariel 6, launched in June 1979, was constructed by Marconi Space & Defence Systems as principal contractor, with BAe providing structures under sub-contract, as well as the cosmic ray experiment payload for the University of Bristol.

During 1966 and 1967 the government had pressed for a further merger within the aircraft industry, but it was not until April 1977 that BAC, the Hawker Siddeley Group (aviation and dynamics), and Scottish Aviation were nationalised and merged as the statutory corporation British Aerospace (BAe). In 1979 BAe officially joined Airbus – the UK having previously withdrawn support for the consortium in 1969 – and the A320 wing work undertaken by Hawker Siddeley ultimately transferred to Filton. The corporation was de-nationalised and changed to a public limited company in June 1981. Management and trade unions worked together during the 1990s to try and secure support for Airbus work at Filton, and in 1997 lobbied the Government to procure the A400M as FLA (Future Large Aircraft). When BAE Systems was created in 1999, it inherited BAe's share in Airbus, which it sold in 2006 – thus ending the UK-owned interest in civil airline production.

BAC was the prime contractor for the world's first geostationary scientific spacecraft, with Filton engineers responsible for the programme of assembly, testing, and launch activities. When the GEOS satellite was launched in April 1977, it failed to achieve the planned orbit, but a second satellite was successfully launched, as GEOS 2, in July 1978. The facility built for testing GEOS in a 'clean' electromagnetic environment survives within the BAE Systems site at Golf Course Lane, Filton.

The Giotto spacecraft was ESA's (European Space Agency) first deep space probe and the first spacecraft to provide close observations of a comet. BAe was appointed as the prime contractor, and also undertook the reaction control system (RCS) to manage the craft's thrusters. Giotto was launched in July 1985 and passed within 400 miles (889 km) of Halley's Comet in March 1986, returning photographs of the nucleus. Set on a new trajectory, the spacecraft came within 125 miles (200 km) of Comet Grigg-Skjellerup in July 1992 and returned further useful data.

Post-Concorde

After the final Concorde left Filton in June 1980, the AAH provided facilities for a variety of projects, some of which had started in the late 1970s. Nine former airline Vickers VC-10 aircraft were converted into aerial refuelling tankers for the RAF between 1977 and 1984; five more were treated similarly in the early 1990s. BAe Aviation Services established a maintenance facility in the AAH in the 1990s, servicing Airbus A300 and A310 and other aircraft, and also converting A300s to cargo aircraft. By 2001 Airbus had assembled some 400 centre fuselage sections for the BAe 146 (later Avro RJ and RJX) regional at Filton.

Aero engines being produced at Patchway by Rolls-Royce in the 1990s included the Pegasus, RB199, and Adour. The three-spool Turbo-Union RB199 resulted from a collaboration with German and Italian companies and was flight tested below the Vulcan test bed aircraft in 1972. It powers the Panavia Tornado swing-wing combat aircraft that entered service in 1979. Filton built some of the cockpits and wings for the Tornado. The Adour was developed in partnership with the French company Turbomeca. It powered the BAE Systems Hawk advanced trainer aircraft, which replaced the Red Arrow team's Gnat aircraft. Development of the EJ200 engine began in the late 1980s through a collaboration that created Eurojet Turbo. The EJ200 powers the Eurofighter Typhoon aircraft, which first flew in 2003.

In 1977, BAC's Electronic & Space Systems Group at Filton was awarded a contract for the development of solar arrays for a planned space telescope. BAC also led a consortium to develop a photon detector instrument as part of the Faint Object Camera. This joint ESA and NASA project was later named after the astronomer Edwin Hubble, and launched via Space Shuttle in April 1990. Two sets of 25-ft (7.6 m) solar arrays – the 'wings' that generate electricity from solar cells – were designed and manufactured by BAe. The second set was a replacement taken to the Hubble in December 1993 as part of a servicing mission.

Cluster was a constellation of four ESA satellites intended to fly in variable formations to gather three-dimensional data on the Earth's electromagnetic fields and particle distributions. BAe at Filton was awarded a sub-contract to produce four RCS propulsion systems. The first four Cluster craft were lost during the maiden launch of the Ariane 5 rocket in June 1996, which failed to achieve orbit due to a

The EJ200 engine is produced at Rolls-Royce for the twin-engine Eurofighter Typhoon multirole fighter. Over 1,100 EJ200 engines have been delivered. (Rolls-Royce plc)

computer software error. The rochet and disintegrated under the resulting extreme aerodynamic forces. The Filton site (by then under MMS) produced four more RCS sets for a replacement Cluster II constellation. These were successfully launched in pairs in July and August 2000.

Matra Marconi Space (MMS) was established in 1990 as a joint venture between the space and telecoms divisions of Matra Espace and Marconi Space Systems (GEC Group). In July 1994 MMS acquired British Aerospace Space Systems (of BAe Dynamics), but at the end of 1997 MMS announced that it intended to close its Filton operations in August 1999. It planned to transfer three-quarters of the 400 staff at Filton to Stevenage, but most took posts with other Bristol-based aerospace companies or set up their own space-related businesses and consultancies. BAe regained an interest in the company when it merged with GEC's Marconi Electronic Systems to form BAE Systems in November 1999.

The MMS site at Filton was prime contractor for the European Polar Platform Envisat Earth environmental monitoring spacecraft and, in 1999, when Filton space operations ended, Envisat was in the middle of its assembly and test programme. A full team decamped to the European Space Technology Centre in Noordwijk, Netherlands, where testing continued. When the Envisat satellite was launched in March 2002, it was the world's largest civilian Earth observation satellite and one of the most sophisticated.

High-technology space work continues in the Bristol area; for example, Systems Engineering & Assessment Ltd (SEA) was awarded an ESA contract in 2011 for a lunar dust analysis package at its Aero-Space Division in north Bristol. In June 2014 SEA was purchased by Thales Alenia and is now part of a major international player in propulsion and satellite systems. Meanwhile, Filton-produced space hardware is currently in orbits around the sun and Earth, and Beagle 2 (for which the first designs were developed by Filton engineers) rests on the surface of Mars. In fact, the last Filton space product remained in storage for nearly twenty years after Filton's space operations closed. The Microwave Humidity Sounder instrument onboard the MetOp C spacecraft was removed from storage in 2017 by the prime contractor in Germany to be prepared for a planned launch in 2018.

European developer and manufacturer of missiles MBDA was created in December 2001 by bringing together the main missile systems companies in France, Italy, and the UK. Through a previous merger this also included BAe Dynamics. MBDA has a systems and software department at Filton.

Rolls-Royce and Airbus

Following demolition of the West Works in 1995, and the clearing of East Works in 2009, aero engine production is now concentrated on the Gipsy Patch Lane site, which is home to Rolls-Royce's Defence Aerospace business. The Adour and EJ200 engines continue to be built, but the Pegasus is no longer in production. The company's current STOVL system is the Rolls-Royce LiftFan, installed in the Lockheed Martin F35B Lightning II joint strike fighter. A new operations factory producing turbines and other components and an engine factory were in use by the end of 2007, together with investments in new training, a restaurant, and office spaces. Rolls-Royce has since invested in a new facility at Patchway to repair and maintain the Airbus A400M's TP400 turboprop engines. The TP400 is produced by the Europrop International consortium, which Rolls-Royce is a member of. The MTR390 turboshaft engine, originally developed to power the Tiger helicopter, is also assembled at Patchway.

Airbus, with its headquarters in Toulouse, France, supplies about half of all worldwide orders for commercial airliners with 100 or more seats. Its UK sites at Filton and Broughton, North Wales, are integral to the design and production of their aircraft. The factory at Broughton assembles wings for the entire family of Airbus commercial aircraft. The Filton site occupies most of that used by British & Colonial and its successors, continuing a century-long tradition of innovative aerospace development at the location. Around 4,000 people are employed in a range of research, design, engineering, and test activities, including over 1,600 engineers covering wing design for all Airbus aircraft and research projects for future aircraft. Filton has been responsible for the design of every Airbus wing since development of the A320. In addition to wing design, the Filton site is also responsible for the design integration of landing gear and fuel systems, and undertakes wing assembly for the A400M military transport aircraft.

Above: A recent view of the Rolls-Royce site at Patchway looking east. Nearly all of the Gipsy Patch Lane site is occupied, with earlier test facilities alongside substantial new buildings. The East Works, on the extreme right, has since been demolished. (Rolls-Royce plc)

Below: Four sets of wings are in different stages of manufacture in the Airbus A400M facility at Filton, which is seen in August 2013. (Airbus)

The A400M multirole transport plane – designed to replace older aircraft such as the Lockheed C-130 Hercules, which serves with the RAF – made its first flight from Seville, Spain, in December 2009. The wings for the A400M are some of the most technically complex parts of the aircraft. The main structure is the wing box, which consists of pre-assembled leading and trailing edges made of composite spars, metallic ribs, and 65.5-ft-long (20 m) composite wing skins. When assembled the wings are fully equipped and transported by road to the Royal Portbury Dock, near Bristol, for shipping to St Nazaire in France. From St Nazaire, they are flown by Airbus A300-600ST Super Transporter (or 'Beluga') to the final assembly line in Seville.

Airbus facilities allow complete landing gear and fuel systems to be tested in near real flight conditions, including extremes of temperature and altitude. For landing gear systems, this can include simulating up to 5,000 flights. The fuel test facility is also used in the development of more environmentally friendly alternatives to kerosene. The wind tunnel, though dating back originally to 1956, has been refurbished and continues to be used to test three-dimensional models of new aircraft and modifications to existing ones. The tunnel is equipped with a 22-ft-diameter (6.7 m), seven-blade carbon fibre fan, driven by a 1.6 MW electric motor that creates wind speeds of up to Mach 0.26 or over 200 mph (322 km/h). The test models are made in-house using modern techniques, including CATIA (computer aided design tool) and additive layer manufacturing from plastic resin and metal products.

In December 2013, the £70 million Airbus Aerospace Park office complex was opened. The facility brings together over 2,300 staff to work on projects such as the new A320neo (new engine option) airliner. Several ranges of 1930s and 1940s

The landing gear for an Airbus A350-1000 wide-body airliner is seen from the control room of the landing gear test rig building at Filton in December 2016. (Airbus)

The Airbus site at Filton seen looking north-west, in November 2013, can be compared with the similar aerial view in 1952 (page 43). Pegasus House is dwarfed by Airbus's Barnwell House. (Airbus)

erection sheds and workshops survive within the Airbus site; these include buildings that were at one time associated with the now-demolished Rodney Works. One of these workshops, together with a then adjacent Bellman hangar, was occupied by the drop tank project during the late 1950s.

A new research and test facility – the Airbus Wing Integration Centre, currently being constructed on the site of the former Rodney Works – is due to open in 2018. The centre will house engineers involved with early-stage research through to in-service aircraft improvements, alongside teams focusing on new technologies. Airbus, together with GKN Aerospace and Rolls-Royce, is a member of the National Composites Centre that opened at Emersons Green, South Gloucestershire, in 2011.

In 2003 GKN Aerospace became a major partner to Airbus on its A380 airliner programme, contributing wing design and supplying major parts of composite wing trailing edges. Five years later GKN acquired the Airbus wing manufacturing facility at Filton and began operations in January 2009 with a dedicated composite manufacturing resource. Production includes precision mechanical components, major sub-assemblies, leading and trailing edges, as well as ribs and pylons for a range of Airbus aircraft. GKN's factory at Severn Beach, South Gloucestershire, uses automatic fibre placement machines to manufacture the complex shapes of composite wing spars. GKN has also made a major investment in production facilities to provide titanium structures for the F-35 Lightning II strike aircraft for BAE Systems.

Chapter 2

Parnall

Parnall & Sons

The Parnall story – or perhaps stories, as there were three separate Parnall companies associated with the aviation industry – is rather complicated and to start we must go back to the nineteenth century.

In 1820, John Parnall began trading as a tinplate manufacturer in Bristol. His sons later set up on their own as tinplate workers, but soon expanded into ironmongery and hardware. In 1839 they began making weighing machines, as well as weights and measures; this part of the business was run by another son, Henry Parnall. In 1845 Henry transferred weighing machine manufacturing to Narrow Wine Street, which became the company headquarters. In 1863 the firm, headed by Henry, began calling itself Parnall & Sons, and in 1877 a foundry was built in Fishponds, Bristol, and a shop fitting department was set up.

Henry's son John took control of the business in 1885, which became a limited liability company in 1889 with John acting as managing director. By the 1880s Parnall & Sons Ltd was the largest shop fitting company in England, with showrooms in Narrow Wine Street and Fairfax Street, weighing scale works in Fishponds, and branches in London and Swansea. By 1893 the business was employing 400 workers and had acquired an iron and brass foundry in Rosemary Street and a steam-powered joinery in Fairfax Street. Shopfront products included high-class glasswork and iron architecture. The weighing machine manufacturer W. & T. Avery took over the company in 1898, but the Parnall name was retained for trading purposes. As a result of the Avery takeover, scale-making by Parnall had been phased out by 1913. The foundry in Fishponds was later sold to George Adlam & Sons Ltd, iron founders and brewer's engineers, and the building survives in Parnall Road.

By the beginning of the First World War, when the company was asked to manufacture naval aircraft, John's son George Parnall (1873–1936) was managing director. To fulfil the Admiralty contracts additional premises in Bristol were acquired, at the Coliseum Works (Park Row), Mivart Street (Easton), and Quakers Friars, and in Belmont Road, Brislington. Over 600 aircraft were constructed during

The Coliseum seen around 1912 before its use by Parnall & Sons. The Coliseum had been used for a wide range of entertainments, some of which apparently continued in parts of the building while aeroplanes were constructed. (Author's Collection)

1914–1918, mostly at the Coliseum Works. The Coliseum had previously been used as an exhibition hall, cinema, skating rink and dance hall. The level wooden floors of former roller-skating rinks proved to be an ideal surface for building and manoeuvring aircraft, as had been discovered by other manufacturers of this period, such as by Sopwith and Handley Page.

The Easton factory concentrated on propeller production and the factory at Brislington mainly on experimental work until propeller work was transferred there in 1916. The Quakers Friars site in central Bristol was used for covering and doping aircraft components. Apart from two of their own designs, Parnall constructed aircraft to the designs of Avro, Fairey Aviation, and Short Bros. The company's head office in 1918 was at the Mivart Street works.

Parnall's chief designer from 1917 was Harold Bolas (1888–1956), who was at first loaned from the Admiralty, where he had been involved with detail design work on the AD Navyplane with help from Reginald Mitchell (1895–1937) of Supermarine. Bolas had previously worked for the Royal Aircraft Factory, Farnborough, making modifications to army airships until his RNAS commission in 1914. The first aircraft Bolas designed for Parnall was the wooden monocoque Panther – a two-seater biplane for the Royal Navy. The fuselage of the Panther was hinged for storage onboard a ship, but tests of the aircraft in 1918 were disappointing and its performance was

Above: Carpentry work dominates this view inside the Coliseum. The aircraft fuselage is possibly for a Short 827 two-seat reconnaissance floatplane, of which Parnall built at least twenty during 1915 to 1916. (Courtesy of Bristol Reference Library)

Below: This Parnall Panther naval biplane was contracted to be built by the British & Colonial Aeroplane Co. but was clearly assembled by Parnall at their Coliseum Works around 1920. (Courtesy of Bristol Reference Library)

little better than the Sopwith 1½ Strutter, which it was intended to replace. Over 300 Panthers were nevertheless ordered but, due to friction between Avery and the Air Ministry, only around thirty seem to have manufactured by Parnall.

George Parnall & Co.

At the end of the war the parent company wanted to return to making shop fittings and equipment and were not convinced of the benefits of retaining an interest in aviation works, although they had by then built 870 aircraft. George Parnall resigned

The Mivart Street factory used by Parnall in Easton accommodated a range of machine tools making metal aeroplane components during the latter part of the First World War. The building survives, in use by a car service business, and is seen here in March 1998. (Author)

in 1919, established his own business – George Parnall & Co. – in 1920 with a few of his previous employees, and leased the Coliseum Works. Bolas accepted Parnall's invitation to join him and built the new company's first design – the Puffin, an experimental amphibious fighter-reconnaissance biplane – alongside the continuing manufacture of shop-fittings. This was followed by the Plover biplane in 1922, and in 1923 the Possum triplane. At this time their aircraft were test-flown from the aerodrome at Filton, having been towed tail-first and wingless behind a lorry from the Coliseum Works. With increased work, the Mivart Street and Quakers Friars premises were re-used and a further works at Feeder Road, Bristol, was acquired for making metal components. As well as office accommodation at the Coliseum, Parnall opened others in Oxford Street, London, and Berkeley Square, Bristol.

Faced with the limitations of his various works in Bristol, Parnall sought other premises. In 1924 he acquired a former aircraft repair depot in Yate, south Gloucestershire. This had been built during 1916–1917 by German prisoners of war, from a POW camp near Westerleigh Common, but had been abandoned since April 1920. Four timber and asbestos flight sheds alongside a small aerodrome had been opened in June 1917 as the Western Aircraft Repair Depot. This was part of an attempt to reduce the total losses of aircraft damaged in combat, which the previous year had been running at two-thirds. An engine repair section was opened in October

From an original drawing by S.J. Loxton
in the County Reference Library, Bristol.

This drawing by Samuel Loxton shows the No. 3 (Western) Aircraft Repair Depot at Yate while still in operation in 1920. (Courtesy of Bristol Reference Library)

1917, comprised of brick-built workshops and test beds in the south-east corner of the 193-acre (78-hectare) site. Renamed No. 3 (Western) Aircraft Repair Depot in March 1918, up to 1,270 men and 498 women were employed at the site. As many as 250 aircraft may have been rebuilt, or new ones created using serviceable parts from damaged ones, at Yate during the First World War.

Within the site was Poole Court, a grand family home built in the 1870s and by 1879 occupied by members of the Hill family of Bristol shipbuilders. During the First World War the house had been used as an officers' mess by the RFC, but had remained empty after the hostilities until it was acquired by Parnall and used for his design staff. Poole Court survives as a valuable community resource, sympathetically restored and used by Yate Town Council. Parnall's relocation to Yate was probably a catalyst for the future development of industrial activity in the town.

George Parnall's company had been closely involved with the light aeroplane movement from the beginning, when it built its first Pixie low-wing monoplane. This had won the Abdulla speed prize at the Light Aircraft Trials at Lympne, Kent, in 1923. This was followed in 1924 by the Mk II Pixie and Imp prototype of 1927. This experience of light aeroplanes was used in developing the two-seat Elf. This touring biplane was Bolas' last design for Parnall and used a box-type fuselage of plywood with spruce members. Warren girder-type wing bracing, similar to that on the Peto, was used rather than wires. Easily converted to seaplane configuration, it was also

The two Mk III Parnall Pixies were monoplanes with detachable upper wings that could also be flown as biplanes. The first of the two, seen here, had a Bristol Cherub flat-twin engine. (Courtesy of Yate and District Heritage Centre)

claimed to have the smallest folded dimensions of any kind in its class. Its narrow width when folded, of 7 ft 11 in. (2.7 m), was intended to facilitate transport through gateways following a forced landing in a field. The prototype Elf was displayed at the International Aero Exhibition in 1929. Parnall set up facilities to build the Elf in quantity on a production line basis with assembly jigs, but the aircraft could not compete with the popular de Havilland D.H.60 Tiger Moth and only two more were completed by 1932.

One of the more unusual aircraft built by Parnall was the Peto – a small reconnaissance biplane with folding wings. The Peto was designed in response to an Air Ministry specification for an aircraft that could be operated from a submarine. One of the Bristol Burney X-type hydroplanes had been designed to do this. Two prototypes of this floatplane made their first flights in 1925 and 1928 and both undertook sea trials with the First World War submarine *M.*2, being carried in a watertight hangar on the deck. The Peto was launched from the submarine by a compressed air catapult and recovered after landing on the sea by a derrick. The *M.*2 sank with the first Peto in 1932 and, although the aircraft was recovered, it was beyond repair. The second prototype was sold for private use in 1934 and its ultimate fate is unknown. The Perch naval training aeroplane of 1926 was another prototype that did not go into production; it could be flown as either a floatplane or landplane. Two contracts from the Air Ministry, for construction or refurbishment of thirty de Havilland D.H.9A military biplanes, during 1926 and 1927, helped keep the workforce busy.

Bolas continued to design aircraft of fabric-covered wooden airframes with strut and wire-braced wings, until the prototype naval reconnaissance Pike of 1927. This used a fuselage framework of steel tubing covered in fabric, but the wings retained a wooden structure. Also in 1927, two autogiros were built at Yate for the Cierva Autogiro Co. The Pipit naval fighter of 1928 had a fabric-covered all-metal fuselage of Duralumin (an early type of age-hardening aluminium alloy) and stainless steel.

Bolas left the company in 1929 and moved to the USA where he was involved with the STOL Dragonfly project, which successfully flew in April 1934 but was abandoned in 1937 due to lack of funding. Bolas returned to the UK in 1940 and worked for Lancashire Aircraft Corporation and later worked with Douglas Pobjoy on the possible use of Rotol products in rotorcraft. Pobjoy and Parnall had a short-lived engine partnership in 1928. H. V. Clarke succeeded Bolas as chief designer at Parnall.

The Hendy 302 was a monoplane to an advanced design by Basil Henderson (1902–1955), founder of Hendy Aircraft and previously on the technical staff of A. V. Roe. Parnall built just one in 1929, which was subsequently rebuilt with a more powerful engine. Another one-off venture was the Parnall Prawn, built during 1930. This was a very small experimental flying boat designed to investigate the effects of placing the engine in the prow of the 'boat'. Many components were made from stainless steel to prevent corrosion by sea water. The 65 hp (48 kW) Ricardo engine

The first Parnall Pipit prototype naval fighter crashed during its official trials in October 1928. The second Pipit, seen here, carried the same serial number and was fitted with a horn-balance on the rudder. This aircraft also crashed, in February 1929. (Air Ministry original via Jet Age Museum)

was mounted on a pivot so that it could be raised to prevent spray being thrown up as the aircraft accelerated over water. The arrangement was not taken up by the Air Ministry!

The Yate works of the 1930s were evidently well-equipped for constructing aircraft of the period, with a carpenter's shop, saw mill, dope shop, trimming shop, fitting and machine shops, treatment plants, stores, and an engine test bed. Around 200 people were employed at this time and components were still being produced at the Coliseum Works. It seems that the Mivart Street, Quakers Friars, and Feeder Road premises were given up in 1925 on the move to Yate. Cabinet-making continued alongside the aircraft work and provided an often much-needed, regular source of income.

Two experimental monoplanes, named Parnall Parasol, were completed to study wing behaviour in flight. Readings were taken from a dynamometer attached to the parasol wing, which was supported above the fuselage but not attached directly to it. Both aircraft were sent to the RAE, Farnborough, in 1930.

The single Miles M.1 Satyr aerobatic biplane, designed by Frederick Miles (1903–1976) and his wife Blossom, born as Maxine Forbes-Robertson (1901–1984), first flew in August 1932. Construction by Parnall was supervised by Mr and Mrs Miles. Of the ninety-four aircraft built at Yate by George Parnall's company, twenty-four were Percival Gull Fours (including the prototype), and so it was the most successful civil aircraft production run. These three-seat monoplanes were designed by Edgar Percival (1897–1984). Construction was from plywood with plywood skinning, with an enclosed cabin. Coming in 1933, the contract came at a time when there were few other orders.

Although Parnall was contracted to provide military aircraft for the Air Ministry, apart from a small batch of Plover naval fighters none of their designs reached full production status. Most Parnall-designed aircraft were used for experimental purposes, except for a few civil aircraft. With dwindling work, the east end of the site, including Poole Court, was sold to Newman Electric Motors in 1932 and Parnall concentrated activity on land alongside the railway line on the west side. The Coliseum Works was also given up at the same time, and returned to its pre-war use as a cinema and dance hall. In 1934 Gardiner Sons & Co. Ltd carried out building work to provide an ice rink within the Coliseum, which opened that year. The Coliseum

The skeletal structure of the sole Parnall G.4/31 general-purpose biplane, which was built to Air Ministry specification and was powered by a Bristol Pegasus engine. (Courtesy of Yate and District Heritage Centre)

was mostly destroyed during a Second World War air raid on 24 November 1940, but the Park Row façade remained largely intact and survives as part of the University of Bristol's Merchant Venturers School of Engineering of 1996; this in turn had replaced the School of Veterinary Science, which had been built on the site in 1948.

By 1935 the only aeroplane at Yate was the fabric-covered G.4/31 general-purpose biplane, which despite its metal structure was already obsolete. Believing that the government's expansion of the RAF would require his works for aviation contracts, George Parnall sold the Yate site to Nash & Thompson Ltd in 1935 and retired. He was not to enjoy a long retirement as he died in 1936 following a stroke.

Parnall Aircraft

Nash & Thompson, established in 1929 by racing car driver A. G. Frazer Nash (1889–1965) and Esmonde Grattan Thompson (1885–1960), had developed a hydraulically powered aircraft gun turret at its works in Tolworth, Surrey. The patent rights, processes, and designs of this company, those of George Parnall & Co., and of the Hendy Aircraft Co. (established at Shoreham, Sussex, in 1929), were combined to form the new company Parnall Aircraft Ltd in May 1935. Henderson became the chief aircraft designer, but the new company's priority was the installation of Frazer-Nash power-assisted gun turrets in sixty-two Hawker Demon two-seat fighter aircraft.

The Hendy Heck (initially Hendy 3308) was built by Westland Aircraft in Yeovil in 1934 for Whitney Straight to a design by Henderson. This two-seat cabin monoplane used spruce and plywood skinning and was renamed the Parnall Hendy Heck when transferred to Yate. It formed the prototype for six Parnall Heck 2C aircraft, which were completed by 1936. The last aircraft to carry the Parnall name was the Type 382 (Heck Mk III) of 1938, but it did not go into production and only one prototype was constructed.

By May 1936 the works at Yate had been re-organised with a new entrance and the drawing office relocated to a new two-storey building, which later became the gun turret training school. A small tool room was also set up in 1936; these facilities expanded until, in 1940, up to eighty toolmakers were producing gauges, jig fixtures, press tools and special-purpose machines for use throughout the works.

In 1938 and 1939 Parnall undertook sub-contract work for the RAF and facilities were expanded to deal with increased orders for gun turrets, including a new assembly shop. The new shop accommodated a moving assembly line, with turrets being pushed from one operation to the next on trolleys. The whole turret system was operated by vane oil motors, powered by high-pressure hydraulic fluid, which were made at the Ridge satellite works in Yate. Promotional literature for hydraulic turrets carried the catchphrase, 'More power to your elbow!' Parnall also developed sophisticated equipment for manufacturing the necessary pipework.

Parnall Aircraft Ltd built the canteen at Yate, around 1939, to meet the needs of its growing workforce. This view shows it in March 1998 when still part of the then Creda factory. (Author)

Workforce shortages led to the employment of more women and the introduction of automatic machinery. Other developments at Yate just before the Second World War included a new canteen with facilities for 200 employees, but even this could not accommodate all the war-time workers in one lunch sitting. The drawing office was also relocated once again.

Aircraft were also assembled for the RAF at Yate in the erecting shop at the southern end of the site. The Armstrong Whitworth Whitley twin-engine medium bomber, introduced in 1937, still made much use of canvas-covering in its construction, despite some metal cladding, and the dope shop had to be extended to carry out this work. This section was dominated by female workers who stitched the fabric coverings and applied the plasticised lacquer by brush, which stiffened and waterproofed the covering. The tailplane for the first Armstrong Whitworth Ensign airliner, which first flew in early 1938, was also constructed at Yate.

By mid-1940, the works had become a major manufacturer of twin and quadruple machine gun turrets, alongside the Nash & Thompson factory at Tolworth. The works was yet again extended and rearranged with new production facilities, including a machine tool section making lathes and milling machines. A new company – Magnall Products – was established in a purpose-built factory at Warmley, south Gloucestershire, to produce light alloy die-cast turret components. Magnall was employing 2,000 staff at the end of the war.

Above: Wing components for Supermarine Spitfire fighter aircraft were assembled in the Parnall factory at Yate during the Second World War. (Courtesy of Yate and District Heritage Centre)

Below: This view of the Yate site around 1950 shows the full extent of the Parnall Aircraft works as it would have been at the end of the Second World War. (Courtesy of Yate and District Heritage Centre)

One of two purpose-built dispersal factories at Temple Cloud, Somerset, built following the air raids on the Yate factory. This is the entrance to one, erected in a quarry, seen in June 1998; it has latterly been used by a circus arts group. (Author)

The Luftwaffe recognised the works as being a strategically important manufacturing site (most Avro Lancaster bombers were equipped with Parnall gun turrets), and carried out two air raids in February and March of 1941. These resulted in the loss of fifty-five lives and considerable damage to the factory. Production was dispersed to at least twenty-two temporary sites with much of the usable equipment and production machinery going to Boulton Mills near Dursley, Gloucestershire. Semi-permanent satellite factories were then established at sites elsewhere in Gloucestershire, Bristol, and Somerset, including a boot factory and a soap works, as well as purpose-built facilities.

Later in the war, a modern factory occupying some 325,000 sq. ft (30,200 sq m) was built on the site of the bombed-out works at Yate, which was completed at the end of 1944. These buildings lasted until 1988 when demolished to make way for a housing estate. The production of nose and tail gun turrets for Lancaster bombers and Short Sunderland flying boats, dorsal turrets for Blackburn Botha torpedo bombers, airframes for Supermarine Spitfire fighters, components for Avro Lincoln bombers, and later parts for Gloster Meteor jet fighters, at the Yate and satellite sites, involved around 10,000 people at its peak. The rebuilt factory at Yate employed 3,500 people.

Immediately after the war the company abandoned the aircraft industry, despite having been one of the largest Spitfire airframe sub-contractors, and switched to

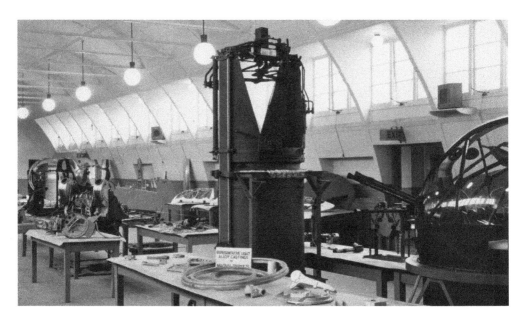

An exhibition of Parnall products in the canteen at Yate in 1945 after the war included several types of gun turret, and alloy castings made by Magnall Products. (Courtesy of Yate and District Heritage Centre)

domestic appliance production trading as Parnall (Yate) Ltd. The company became part of the Radiation Group in 1958, which broadened the range of domestic appliances. In 1967 Radiation was taken over by Tube Investments Ltd, and in 1972 Parnall (Yate) Ltd was renamed Jackson Electric, and the Parnall name was finally lost in Yate. Parts of the works, including two of the 1917 hangars and a security block, remain within the former Parnall site, now part of the Whirlpool Corporation.

Parnall & Sons, Fishponds

But this is not the end of the Parnall story, for while George Parnall & Co. was busy establishing itself at Yate, the Avery Group (still trading under the name of Parnall & Sons) had relocated in 1923 to the former Brazil Straker site at Fishponds (vacated by Cosmos Engineering's move to become part of the Bristol Aeroplane Company). Parnall & Sons was later awarded Air Ministry contracts during the period of RAF re-armament, which took place alongside the manufacture of shop-fittings, refrigerated display and cold storage cabinets, and office furniture. Air Ministry work included construction of wings for de Havilland Tiger Moth biplanes and Airspeed Oxford monoplane trainers, and fuselages for Airspeed Horsa gliders.

Further contracts were undertaken at the Fishponds site during the Second World War, including components for Airspeed, Bristol, Fairey, de Havilland, Handley Page,

A view inside the Parnall factory at Fishponds in June 1954 shows components for the Bristol Type 175 Britannia being made under contract. (Reproduced under licence from and courtesy of BAE SYSTEMS)

The entrance in Goodneston Road to part of the former Parnall & Sons works in Fishponds, in February 1998 while some of the factory was still in mixed business use. (Author)

and Short Bros. aircraft. After the war, the company's metal fabrication abilities and woodworking skills continued to be used to supply the aircraft industry. Parnall assembled wooden fuselages for de Havilland Venom jet fighters (1952), tailplanes for de Havilland Herons, and interior fittings for the de Havilland Comet airliner (1955), and metal parts for the Hawker Siddeley 125 corporate jet (1965). Interior furnishings were also provided for Bristol Britannia airliner until 1960, including plastic components, and for the mock-up and prototype Concorde aircraft. Much of this work was carried out in a building known as Shed 49 at the Filwood Road/Goodneston Road end of the site. This was at first separate from the main building, but was incorporated during building work in the early 1950s. The distinctive square chimney that was in the north-west corner of the site appears to date from this period.

By 1970 Parnall occupied an irregular site bounded by Lodge Causeway, Goodneston Road, Filwood Road, Parnall Road, and the Bristol–Gloucester railway line. This evidently included parts of the former Avonside locomotive works, but not the foundry (built by Parnall & Sons). Parnall & Sons was bought by GEC in 1979 and was subsequently sold to C. H. Holdings; the company finally went out of business in May 1991 following losses made by its parent company and two factory fires. The original offices of Brazil Straker were demolished soon after in 1992.

The remaining Fishponds site of 6.35 acres (2.57 hectares) was offered for sale in 1999, including 150,000 sq. ft (13,935 sq. m) of buildings, by which time the site was variously occupied by businesses associated with the motor trade.

Most of the buildings associated with the aircraft industry at Fishponds are now demolished and the site has been given over to an industrial and trading estate or left redundant. The final aviation connection appears to have been the occupation of the adjacent former Weber chocolate factory by Diamonite Aircraft Furnishings from around 2000 to produce high-class aircraft interiors. In September 2001 Diamonite were contracted to refurbish the Russian presidential Ilyushin IL-96-300 four-engine airliner, which was completed in 2003, together with interiors for two Mil-8 VIP helicopters for the presidential airline. The company employed between sixty and 120 staff and refurbished interiors for over forty Russian aircraft, as well as providing interior dividers and wardrobes for Airbus. Diamonite was incorporated as a private limited company in 2005 but dissolved in March 2014.

Chapter 3

Gloucestershire Aircraft Company

H. H. Martyn & Co.

Unlike British & Colonial at Bristol, but similarly to Parnall, the Gloster Aircraft story starts at least partly outside the aviation industry. H. H. Martyn & Co. in Cheltenham (established in 1888 by Herbert Henry Martyn) were originally monumental masons working in stone, marble and wood that had extended to joinery, wrought iron work and castings, and by 1914 included pressed steel. They were well-known for their high-quality craft work at their 5 acres (2 hectares) of workshops, decorating palaces and fitting out ocean liners, and it is for this reason that they were subcontracted by the Aircraft Manufacturing Co. (Airco) during the First World War.

Airco was formed by George Holt Thomas (1869–1929) and started out at Merton (south London), building French Farman-designed aircraft and Gnome aero-engines under licence from 1910 – the engines in collaboration with Peter Hooker (1817–1902) at his factory in Walthamstow, east London. In 1912 Thomas took over hangars at Hendon, which was then part of Middlesex and is now home to the RAF Museum. Hugh Burroughes (1884–1985), who had worked previously at the Royal Aircraft Factory at Farnborough, became Airco's first manager in March 1914. In May of the same year, Geoffrey de Havilland (1882–1965) was recruited, also from Farnborough, as chief designer. His aeroplane designs for the company were given the prefix 'DH'. Airco became a major aircraft manufacturer (in 1918 Holt Thomas claimed it to be the largest in the world) with up to 8,000 employees, but could not meet all the wartime demands. When Holt's post-war civil aviation business failed, Airco was sold to the BSA group in 1920, from which de Havilland bought the aircraft manufacturing assets to set up his own company (de Havilland Aircraft Co. Ltd).

It was Burroughes who first made contact with H. H. Martyn when Airco needed increased production capacity for their DH.2 single-seat biplane fighter with single pusher propeller. In April 1915 they agreed a contract to produce components for Farman biplanes; this was followed by work on the DH.2. In June 1917, a new

The factory of H. H. Martyn & Co. at Sunningend, west of the railway line in Cheltenham, was the starting point for the Gloucestershire Aircraft Co. (Jet Age Museum Collection)

company – Gloucestershire Aircraft Co. Ltd (GAC) – was formed with £10,000 approved capital (compared to the £25,000 of British & Colonial seven years previously), H. H. Martyn and Airco taking equal shares. Martyn's Sunningend works, near Cheltenham Spa railway station, were rented, and Gloucestershire Aircraft took over Airco's subcontract work from Martyn. By the end of 1917 the company had built 150 Airco DH.6 biplane trainers.

In 1918 a similar number of Bristol Fighter biplanes were completed and GAC had so much work that they in turn were forced to subcontract to other local firms, including Daniels & Co. (Stroud) and the Gloucester Carriage & Wagon Co. They were then building forty-five aeroplanes a week. With no facilities of their own, test flights were carried out at Brockworth Aircraft Acceptance Park (AAP). Completed aircraft were fitted with specially adapted road wheels and towed to the AAP by a lorry, the wings being carried separately.

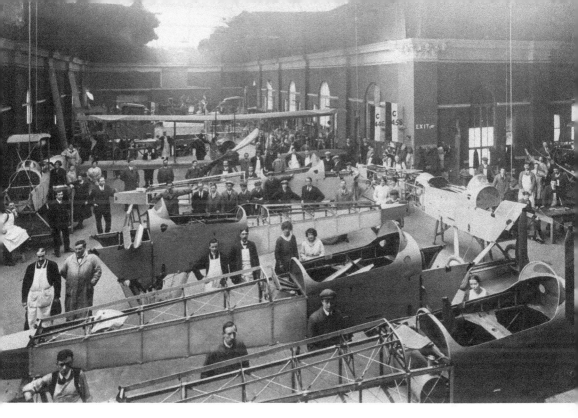

Increasing demand during the First World War caused Gloucestershire Aircraft to take over other premises. Here workers pose next to Airco DH.6 biplanes in various stages of assembly in Cheltenham's Winter Garden Pavilion. (Jet Age Museum Collection)

During the war GAC employed many female workers; some of the work was particularly suited to the domestic skills they already had. Women undertook all the cutting, stitching and fitting of the fabric that covered the wooden frames of the fuselages, tails and wings. Once secured the fabric was treated with dope, so that it stretched tight and strengthened.

At the end of hostilities, GAC was determined to remain in aircraft manufacture, despite the cancellation of military contracts. The rights for the Nighthawk biplane fighter were acquired together with a quantity of components, in part settlement of cancelled contracts. The Nighthawk was designed by Henry Folland (1889–1954) for Nieuport & General Aircraft Co. Ltd towards the end of the war, but its troublesome ABC Dragonfly radial engine led to the cancellation of orders from the RAF. Folland was first engaged by GAC as consulting engineer, and then joined as their chief designer, and converted his Nighthawk into the Mars series of racer and fighter aircraft from 1921. These included the Sparrowhawk and Nightjar.

The Mars I (also known as the 'Bamel') first flew in June 1921 powered by a Napier Lion II engine. The Mars I was modified over time and won the Aerial Derby in three consecutive years, also setting a British speed record of 212 mph (339 km/h). Fitted with a more powerful Lion engine, the aircraft was renamed the Gloster I,

Above: Gloucestershire Aircraft took on female workers to fill vacancies left by men joining the armed services during the First World War. Women are in the majority in the dope shop, where wing sections are being treated. (Jet Age Museum Collection)

Below: The Mars I earned its 'Bamel' nickname when under construction; when only the front of the fuselage was covered and with the hump of the fuel tank it was described by Henry Folland as 'half bare – half camel'. (Jet Age Museum Collection)

Twenty-five Nieuport Nighthawk airframes were converted in 1922 to the Mars VI fighter for the Greek Army Air Force and re-equipped with Armstrong Siddeley Jaguar engines. (Jet Age Museum Collection)

sold to the RAF in 1924, and when fitted with floats was used to train Schneider Trophy Contest pilots.

Derived from the Nighthawk, but using a Bentley BR2 rotary engine, the Sparrowhawk (Mars II, III and IV) were fighters for the Imperial Japanese Navy, which bought fifty aircraft. These became the Sparrowhawk I (land-based naval fighter), Sparrowhawk II (two-seat trainer) and Sparrowhawk III (shipborne fighter). The Nightjar (Mars X) was a similar carrier-based fighter, in service with the RAF from 1922 to 1924; twenty-two were built. The single experimental Grouse was built to try and combine the advantages of monoplanes and biplanes, providing both high lift for take-off but with low drag in flight. Adapted from a Sparrowhawk II, it again used the Bentley BR2 engine. The Grouse was later adapted as a trainer and sold to the Swedish air force in 1926.

The tiny and easily portable Gannet biplane of 1923 was built for the Royal Aero Club light aircraft trials at Lympne in Kent, which limited engine size to 750cc. The Gannet was equipped with a Carden two-cylinder, air-cooled, two-stroke engine of exactly 750cc, designed especially for the trials, but overheating and lubrication problems prevented it from competing.

Racing Seaplanes

A series of racing seaplanes were constructed during 1924 to 1929, the earlier ones being constructed mostly of wood. The Gloster II biplane, powered by a Napier Lion VA twelve-cylinder, water-cooled 'W' engine of 585 hp (436 kW) was a development of the Gloster I. Two were constructed to an Air Ministry order to compete in the 1924 Schneider Trophy race, which had been won the previous year by the US Navy. The first aircraft was ready for testing in September 1924 but on landing its undercarriage collapsed and it sank, though the pilot escaped unhurt. There was not time to prepare the second in time for the competition, which was itself cancelled by the Americans for lack of European entries. The second Gloster II was converted to a landplane and used to test equipment for the Gloster III, but was lost in a high-speed crash-landing in June 1925, which seriously injured the pilot. Two Gloster III seaplanes were built in 1925 for the Schnieider Trophy of the same year, using the more powerful Napier Lion VII engine of 700 hp (522 kW), and like the Gloster II they were wooden biplanes. They first flew in August 1925 and were again built to an Air Ministry contract. One of the aircraft was damaged during taxiing tests on the day of the race, leaving only one to compete, which came second to an American Curtiss R3C that achieved an average speed 33 mph (53 km/h) more than the Gloster aircraft. After the race, the two seaplanes were modified and used for training RAF pilots preparing for the 1927 competition. Three

The Gloster VI was the last of the racing seaplanes, seen here at RAF Calshot, Southampton Water, in 1929. (Jet Age Museum Collection)

Gloster IV seaplanes were constructed for the 1927 race, having slightly different wing and tail arrangements. Only one competed and this had to withdraw due to a cracked propeller shaft. The Gloster VI was the last of the racing seaplanes. It was a monoplane with a semi-monocoque metal fuselage skinned with duralumin, and the wooden wings were covered almost completely with flush-fitting brass surface radiators. The aircraft were described as being among the most beautiful in the world. Folland had to abandon his preference for biplanes when designing the Gloster VI, as it was found impossible to accommodate the super-charged Napier Lion VIID engine. Two Gloster VIs were built for the 1927 Schnieider Trophy competition but both were withdrawn before the race as the Lion engine, now boosted to 1,320 hp (984 kW), proved unreliable when cornering. The race was won by the Supermarine S.6 monoplane, powered by a Rolls-Royce R engine, but the day after one of the Gloster VI aircraft (named *Golden Arrow*) briefly held the outright world speed record at an average of just over 336 mph (537 km/h).

The prototype Grebe was developed from the Grouse, but powered by a 350 hp (260 kW) Armstrong Siddeley Jaguar III radial engine, and the design can be traced back to Folland's Nighthawk of 1919. The Grebe was the first fighter design built in quantity by GAC, and was the first post-First World War fighter aircraft. It entered

Gloster Grebe Mk II fuselages and wings under construction in 1924. The part-completed fuselages include that for serial number J7533, one of 129 Grebes built in five batches between 1923 and 1927. (Jet Age Museum Collection)

service in October 1923 when a flight of No. 111 Squadron was re-equipped. A total of 133 Grebes were built, including four prototypes, and three were sold to the New Zealand air force. In October 1926, two Grebes were adapted to be launched from underneath the R33 airship of 1919.

The Gorcock of 1925 was an experimental single-seat biplane fighter, three were built to develop metal-framed aircraft. The first two had fabric covered steel fuselages and wooden wings, the third had an all-steel airframe and was GAC's first all-metal aircraft. The Gamecock was a development of the Grebe, using a more powerful Bristol Jupiter VI nine-cylinder radial, 425 hp (317 kW) engine instead of the less-reliable Armstrong Siddeley Jaguar, and entered RAF service in 1926. Just over 100 Gamecocks were built, some of which saw service with the Finnish Air Force.

By 1918 the airfield at Brockworth (later known as Hucclecote) covered 140 acres (56.7 hectares) with 20 acres (8.7 hectares) of covered accommodation, including five aeroplane sheds and seven storage sheds. The aeroplane sheds represented the last type of First World War hangar to use timber roof trusses of the Belfast type. Four of these general service sheds were in coupled pairs as Hangars 1 and 2; Hangar 3 was a single shed. It is thought that, as at Yate, the buildings for the AAP were constructed by German prisoners of war in 1918. The site was served by a tramway to bring workers and materials from Gloucester docks.

The Gloucestershire Aircraft Co. had rented part of Hangar 2 from 1921 as a flight shed, but in 1925 began the process of relocating to the by then 200-acre (80.9-hectare)

Hangar 1 was the last of the former AAP sheds to remain at Brockworth, seen here in May 1998 but now demolished. (Author)

site. The works at Sunningend at that time were described as being well laid out for efficient and rapid production, but were becoming less suitable with the gradual move from wood toward metal construction. The whole airfield was purchased in 1928 for £15,000 and the move from Sunningend was completed in 1930.

Gloster Aircraft

By the mid-1920s Gloucestershire Aircraft was well known in Britain, but had also done business in Japan and Finland, having sold aircraft of Sparrowhawk and Gamecock types. The simpler marketing name of Gloster Aircraft Co. was adopted by December 1926, which presented a more easily pronounceable name to potential overseas customers, though to its staff it was known simply as GAC.

Folland continued to develop new aircraft to Air Ministry specifications during the later 1920s, but none proceeded beyond one or two prototypes. These included the Guan experimental high-altitude biplane (1925); Goral general-purpose biplane, which used components from the accumulated stocks of Airco DH.9A parts (1926); Goring day bomber/torpedo biplane (1926); Goldfinch all-metal development of the Gamecock (1927); and Gnatsnapper naval deck-landing fighter (1928). However, 150 Gambet naval deck-landing fighter biplanes were built under licence by the Nakajima Aircraft Co. for the Imperial Japanese Navy and designated as Nakajima

The first of thirty Sparrowhawk I land-based naval fighters ordered by the Imperial Japanese Navy in 1921. (Jet Age Museum Collection)

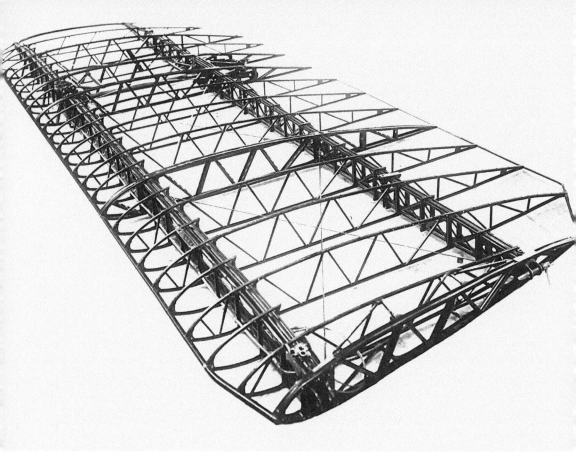

The metal wings for the Gnatsnapper naval fighter prototype were constructed by the Steel Wing Co. (Jet Age Museum Collection)

A1N, or Navy Type 3 Carrier Fighter. A development of the Gamecock fighter, the prototype Gambet was built by Gloster and first flew in December 1927, before being shipped to Japan in early 1928. The A1N was equipped with a Bristol Jupiter engine developed under licence by Nakajima.

Gloster built their new administration and design offices at Brockworth, north-west of Hangars 2 and 3. The former AAP sheds provided accommodation for sheet metal work, copper and tin smiths, erectors and fitters, machine shop, wing assembly, woodworking, and cover and dope shops. A wind tunnel was established in Shop No. 4. Hangar 1 was used as a flight shed in the late 1920s and early 1930s, and then as a materials store.

As the use of metal in aircraft construction increased, Burroughes promoted the development of all-metal airframes. But not all members of Gloster's Board were convinced, especially those from the woodworking tradition of H. H. Martyn, and chairman Alfred W. Martyn (born around 1871) resigned in 1927 (he later became chairman of Aircraft Components Ltd, which we will come back to). In the same year, Howard Saint (1893–1976) joined as chief test pilot. He had served with the

A Gloster Gamecock fighter in flight over one of the former AAP hangars at Brockworth. (*Flight* magazine via Jet Age Museum)

RAF during the First World War and afterwards joined the Airco subsidiary Aircraft Transport & Travel as a commercial pilot, carrying out the first civilian flight after the wartime ban was lifted in May 1919. He re-joined the RAF in 1922, serving for a time as a test pilot, until he was appointed by Gloster. When Saint left in 1935 following the takeover by Hawker Aircraft Ltd (see below), he had flown fourteen Gloster types – more than any of the company's other test pilots. On leaving Gloster he went briefly to George Parnall & Co. until the Yate company moved away from aircraft production.

In August 1926 GAC bought the rights for British Hele-Shaw Beacham variable pitch (v-p) propeller hub, which was test flown on Bristol Jupiter engines in Grebe, Gamecock and Guan biplanes. The v-p rights were later sold to Rotol at Staverton. Another purchase by Gloster was that of the Steel Wing Co. of Hither Green, London, established in 1919 for research into the use of steel in aircraft construction, in 1928. This proved to be an important acquisition, and provided work when there was no aircraft production underway. Contracts were undertaken for Armstrong Whitworth, and 525 sets of metal wings were constructed at Hucclecote for all the

Westland Wapiti general-purpose military single-engine biplanes (originally built with standard wooden DH.9A components) – an order that was worth £360,000. Another welcome contract was for the construction of Armstrong Whitworth Siskin single-seat biplane fighters from 1927. Seventy-four had been built by 1930 and many more repaired.

The largest aircraft built by Gloster was the one-off TC33 bomber-transport biplane designed in response to a Ministry specification. It was the only four-engine aircraft constructed by Gloster. The Rolls-Royce liquid-cooled Kestrel engines were mounted in tandem pairs, in a tractor-pusher arrangement, driving four 12 ft 6 in (3.8 m) diameter propellers. The aircraft was 80 ft (24.3 m) long, had a wing span of 95 ft (28.9 m), stood 25 ft 8 in (7.8 m) high, and had a gross weight of 28,884 lbs (13,101 kg). When completed in January 1932, it was too high to pass through the doors of Hangar 2; trenches had to be dug for the 5-ft-diameter (1.5 m) landing wheels and the aircraft had to be dragged out with a winch borrowed

The TC33 bomber-transport biplane of 1931 was Gloster's only four-engine aircraft. The Rolls-Royce Kestrel engines were mounted in tandem pairs in a tractor-pusher arrangement, driving four propellers. (Jet Age Museum Collection)

from Gloucester Docks. The aircraft did not reach production stage due to its poor performance.

The high-performance Gloster Gauntlet single-seat biplane fighter, powered by the Bristol Mercury VI radial engine, followed in 1933. On entering service with the RAF they were 56 mph (90 km/h) faster than the Bristol Bulldog they replaced, and until 1937 remained the RAF's fastest aircraft. They were also the last open cockpit fighter in service with the RAF and the penultimate biplane. The Gauntlet's fuselage was formed of steel tubing, with spars and ribs of high-tensile stainless steel. Metal panelling was used between the cockpit and the nose but the rear fuselage and wings were fabric-covered.

The development of the Gauntlet and a succession of prototypes that did not reach production status (including the TSR.38 three-seat torpedo/spotter/reconnaissance aircraft) had drained Gloster's resources so much that non-aviation activities were carried out from around 1930 to supplement income. Hangars were rented out for indoor tennis and badminton courts, vehicle storage, pigsties and mushroom cultivation. Production included motorcar bodies, Pittman gas-fired fish fryers, roll-up metal shop fronts, a powered bomb-carrier, and milk churns.

A line-up of Gloster Gauntlet I single-seat fighters from a batch of twenty-four production aircraft built in 1935. (Jet Age Museum Collection)

A powered bomb-carrier trialled in 1934 was an example of Gloster Aircraft's attempts at diversification. Some fifty of the Festing Motorised Barrow were ultimately built for Air Ministry use. (Jet Age Museum Collection)

Hawker Aircraft

This lean period ended when Hawker Aircraft Ltd acquired Gloster in May 1934, and continued to produce aircraft under the Gloster name. The take-over provided extra work as Hawker products were then built alongside their own, including forty-six Hawker Hardy general-purpose biplanes between 1934 and 1935, when no other aircraft were built by Gloster. The Hardy was a variant of the Hawker Hart two-seat light bomber, adapted for use in Iraq as a replacement for the Westland Wapiti. The prototype was a production Hart that was fitted with a modified radiator, a message pick-up hook, water containers and a desert survival kit. Twenty-five Hawker Audax, an army co-operation version of the Hart, were constructed in 1935. Seventy-two Harts had also been built by 1937.

In 1935 Hawker Aircraft merged with Armstrong Siddeley and its subsidiary, Armstrong Whitworth Aircraft, to form Hawker Siddeley Aircraft. This group also included A. V. Roe & Co. (Avro). The Brockworth–Hucclecote parish boundary ran through the built-up area of the site, though the postal address of the company was changed to Hucclecote, which became its official address. It has been suggested that this was because the latter had two postal deliveries a day and Brockworth only one.

One of the best-known Gloster aircraft was the Gladiator; developed from the Gauntlet by Gloster as a private venture, the prototype first flew from Hucclecote in

September 1934. Designated by Gloster as the SS.37, it received its Gladiator name in 1935. It became the last biplane fighter to enter major first-line service work with the RAF, from 1937, and was also the first with an enclosed cockpit, with many seeing active service during the Second World War.

The Gladiator had a metal structure of steel tubing and strip covered in fabric. They were initially powered by the Bristol Mercury IX radial engine, with the Gladiator II receiving the Mercury VIIIA. A total of 747 aircraft were built and, as well as serving with the RAF and a version for the Fleet Air Arm, served with Chinese, Finnish and Norwegian air services among other overseas operators. The Finnish Air Force

The F.5/34 had the appearance of a Gloster Gladiator with the top wing and fixed undercarriage removed. (Late Jim Oughton via Jet Age Museum)

was the last to use the aircraft in combat in 1943, but Gladiators served with the Portuguese Air Force (as it was from 1952) in a secondary role until 1953.

Folland left Gloster following the takeover by Hawker Aircraft, fearing that their designs would be favoured over his. He purchased the British Marine Aircraft Co. at Hamble, near Southampton, and renamed it Folland Aircraft Ltd. His last design for Gloster was the F.5/34 (unofficially the 'unnamed fighter'), the company's first monoplane and the first with a retractable undercarriage. Powered by the Bristol Mercury IX nine-cylinder radial engine of 840 hp (627 kW), it had a top speed of 316 mph (505 km/h). The first of only two prototypes flew in December 1937, by which time the Air Ministry requirement had been met by the Hawker Hurricane. Folland's replacement as chief designer was George Carter (1889–1969), who had joined Gloster in 1931 having worked previously for Sopwith Aviation Co., Hawker Engineering Co. Ltd, Short Bros, de Havilland, and Avro aircraft manufacturers.

During 1936 to 1938 a main office building was constructed at Hucclecote north of the 1918 shops and infilling took place between these earlier sheds. South of the original site, a new erecting shop, the longest of its kind in England at the time, was built during 1937 and 1938. Construction of a shadow (No. 2) factory began to the south-west with site clearance in 1938; it provided a further 24 acres (9.7 hectares) of floor space and was completed in November 1940. This new factory undertook

The final Hawker Typhoon, serial No. SW772, was completed in November 1945 and was paraded before an enthusiastic crowd when it emerged from the factory. (Jet Age Museum Collection)

production of Hurricane fighters, Hawker Typhoon fighter-bombers and Armstrong Whitworth Albemarle transport aircraft; 2,750 Hurricanes and 3,330 Typhoons had been built by 1945. The new No. 2 factory site covered a total of 43 acres (17.4 hectares) and at the beginning of the Second World War provided a combined production area of 1 million sq. ft (92,900 sq. m).

As with other aircraft manufacturers during the war, sections of the factory were relocated to reduce the threat of loss from an enemy air attack. Premises such as a manor house, billiard hall and commercial garages were used. New dispersal factories were created in Bentham (east of Hucclecote – experimental design office & factory); Stoke Orchard and Uckington (both near Cheltenham – assembly & flight shed, and tool room, fitting shop and presses respectively); Newent (Forest of Dean – sheet metal); and Ledbury (Herefordshire – wing assembly). In 1942 the Hucclecote site was provided with a concrete runway and an air control tower of reinforced concrete to the south. No. 3 site was provided with a MAP (Ministry of Aircraft Production) B1-type hangar, and erecting and flight sheds. Peak employment at all of Gloster's sites reached 12,500.

Two women workers attaching fabric covering to the steel frame of a Hawker Hurricane appear to have the attention of VIP visitors. (Second World War press cutting via Jet Age Museum)

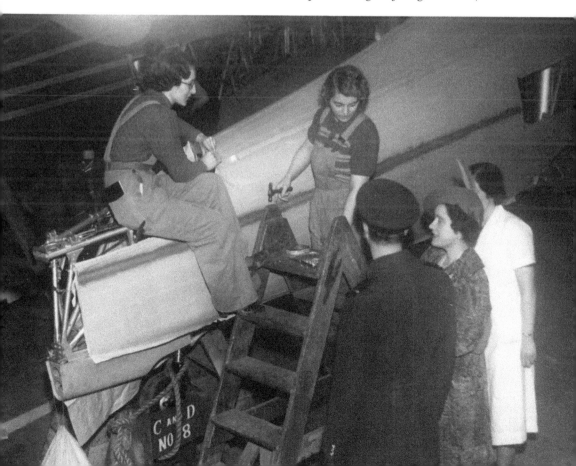

Power Jets

Frank Whittle (1907–1996) had been working on the development of gas turbine aero engines since 1929, but it was not until January 1936 that Whittle set up a company to exploit the potential of turbojet engines. The other parties were Rolf Williams (1908–1987), James Tinling (1900–1983), and investment bankers O. T. Falk & Partners. Power Jets Ltd was incorporated in March the same year, with authorised capital of £10,000 to develop Whittle's jet engine patents.

The task undertaken by Power Jets was long and often frustrating, but Whittle had visited Gloster's works in April 1939 to discuss with Carter production of an experimental aircraft in which to test the flight version of his engine. By July that year Carter had produced initial proposals and the basic design was completed by February 1940. Whittle had hoped that the Air Ministry would place a contract for the aircraft through Power Jets, but it was eventually awarded to Gloster for two prototypes under specification E28/39. Gloster paid Power Jets £500 for their contribution to the design work.

The aircraft was a small, low-wing monoplane of all-metal construction, apart from fabric-covered control surfaces, and tricycle landing gear. Initial work took place in the experimental shop at Hucclecote, but was moved to a dispersal site at Regents Motors, Cheltenham (the site of the Regent Arcade since 1985), due to the threat of air raids. Only the small team concerned with assembling the aircraft knew it was being built. The first prototype, also known as the E28 'Pioneer', was initially fitted with Whittle's WIX engine, which had been constructed from non-airworthy parts and therefore only suitable for ground trials. During taxiing trials on 8 April 1941 the aircraft achieved three short flights of between 300 ft (100 m) and 600 ft (200 m) at Hucclecote. Whether this constituted the first flight of a British jet is debatable, but it was nevertheless a highly significant event. After these tests the aircraft was taken back to Cheltenham – this time to Crabtree's Garage (also known as the Old Post Office Garage) in Carlton Street – for adjustments to be made to the landing gear and the fitting of the Whittle W1 flight engine. The second prototype was also assembled in this building, during 1942 and 1943.

From this garage the aircraft was taken to RAF Cranwell. The Gloster aerodrome had no hard runway at this time and was surrounded by hills; it was also thought it was easier to maintain the project's secret in rural Lincolnshire. The official first flight took place at Cranwell on 15 May 1941 at the hands of Gloster's chief test pilot, P. E. G. ('Jerry') Sayer (1905–1942). After further tests at RAF Edgehill in south Warwickshire, and Farnborough, E28/39 was returned to Gloster's design and experimental unit at Bentham, where a new Power Jets engine was fitted.

The first prototype was sent to the Science Museum in London in 1946, where it is now displayed, without an engine, in the Flight Gallery. The second prototype did not fare so well, being destroyed in a crash caused by an aileron failure while

The W1X engine in the first E28/39 prototype as installed in April 1941 by Robert Feilden of Power Jets. The lines of thermal paint on the fuselage were to monitor the temperature of the airframe. (Air Ministry original via Jet Age Museum)

undertaking high-altitude tests in July 1943. A full-size replica can be seen much nearer the original's birthplace at the Jet Age Museum, near Gloucestershire Airport.

Even before the E28/39 had been flight tested, Gloster was authorised to start the design of a twin-engine jet fighter. Carter realised that it would take time to develop sufficient power in the turbojet for a single-engine fighter so opted for two engines. Eight prototypes to Air Ministry specification F9/40 were produced, powered by a variety of engines from Power Jets, Rover, Metropolitan Vickers, Rolls-Royce and de Havilland. The new aircraft had an all-metal airframe with stressed-skin covering, the fuselage being constructed in three sections. The first flight of the F9/40, which became the Meteor, took place in March 1943, during which a speed of 430 mph (688 km/h) was reached.

A first production batch of twenty Meteors was produced from January 1944. Deliveries to the RAF began in July the same year, so becoming Britain's first jet-powered combat aircraft. Test flying took place at Moreton Valence, originally RAF Haresfield – 5.6 miles (9.0 km) south-west of Gloucester – which had opened

Eight prototype aircraft were ordered in February 1941 to meet specification F.9/40. The third Meteor prototype was powered by two Metropolitan Vickers turbojets in underwing nacelles. It first flew in November 1943 and is seen here at Bentham. (Jet Age Museum/Russell Adams Collection)

in 1939. Armstrong Whitworth Albemarle transports were also tested at Haresfield before its redevelopment and renaming in 1941. By 1943, when Gloster was granted permission to use the airfield as an assembly and test facility, further sheds and a runway extension had been added. The departure of the RAF in October 1946 left Gloster in sole occupation of Moreton Valence.

All 600 of the Armstrong Whitworth A.W.41 Albemarle twin-engine glider-tug and transport aircraft were assembled in No. 2 factory from parts and sub-assemblies supplied by around 1,000 sub-contractors. The work was carried out by A. W. Hawksley Ltd, a subsidiary of Gloster set up for this purpose. The Hawker Siddeley Group, of which Gloster was a part, included Armstrong Whitworth. Post-war diversification saw the No. 2 factory used by Hawksley to build prefabricated bungalows (as did Bristol Aircraft Company), some 18,000 being constructed over a four-year period.

Gloster Javelin

Shortly after the war, the RAF identified the need for heavily armed, radar-equipped, all-weather fighter aircraft. In response to this need Gloster proposed a delta-winged aircraft powered by two jet engines, and in July 1948 received an order for four

The Javelin GA5 prototype is flying over Gloster's Hucclecote factory and Brockworth airfield in 1954. The curved roofs of the Belfast hangars can be seen to the left, beyond other mostly late First World War buildings. Below the aircraft is the No. 2 shadow factory. (Jet Age Museum/Russell Adams Collection)

prototypes to the designation of GA5. Work on this aircraft – later named the Javelin – began at Hucclecote and Bentham in April 1949, with final assembly at Moreton Valence, where the first flight also took place in November 1951. Constructed almost entirely of light alloy, apart from steel edging, it was the world's first operational delta aircraft. At 38,100 lbs (17,282kg) – fifteen times the weight of the Mars I aeroplane forty-three years previously – it was also Gloster's heaviest.

The construction of Meteor and Javelin aircraft carried on alongside each other, until the final Meteor was completed at Brockworth in March 1954. Fuselage sections were moved from stage to stage of the assembly lines on wheeled cradles or carriages and the production line for Javelins was a quarter of a mile (400 m) long. By the end of production, a total of 3,897 Meteors had been built in a number of variants, including production by Armstrong Whitworth, and in Belgium and the Netherlands.

Brockworth Engineering Co. was established by Armstrong Siddeley Motors in 1953 to produce Sapphire jet engines, with No. 2 shadow factory being converted for this purpose. An engine test facility was built toward the south-west of the airfield, comprising two flat-roofed blocks of brick and reinforced concrete that housed ten test beds in pairs. The two test houses were separated by a dozen fuel tanks. Vertical air splitters and heavily insulated detuners were provided to reduce external noise levels.

The final development of the Brockworth/Hucclecote site for aviation industry use was in the mid-1950s. An extension of six bays was built at No. 1 site for Javelin production, immediately south of the 1938 erecting shop. This and a further shop, echoing the design of shops 4 to 10, were completed in March 1955. In 1956 a vast spray paint shop was established in the MAP hangar at No. 3 site, complete with floor extractors and roof fans.

Changing government policy on military aircraft requirements halted Gloster's work on a supersonic fighter project around 1956. Proposals for VTOL and large military transport aircraft and an unmanned crop-spraying helicopter were also abandoned. In an effort to keep the factory working, Gloster took to manufacturing fire engines, road tankers, forage harvesters, industrial sweepers, lighting columns, and even vending machines.

In 1960 the company began a major programme of modifications to Javelin aircraft. A programme of converting Meteor night-fighters to target tugs was also carried out at Moreton Valence. The final Javelin to be built left the Gloster site in April 1960, by which time 435 had been completed. The Javelin remained in service with the RAF until 1968.

Rationalisation of the aircraft industry resulted in the merger of Gloster and Armstrong Whitworth in October 1961 to become Whitworth Gloster Aircraft Co. In July 1963, this company became part of Hawker Siddeley Aviation's Avro Whitworth Division, and in turn became part of British Aerospace in 1977.

Gloster's main Hucclecote factory and airfield was sold to Gloucester Trading Estates in April 1964. The No. 2 site of 1940 passed from A. W. Hawksley to Brockworth Engineering (part of the Hawker Siddeley Group producing jet engines), and was then taken over by British Nylon Spinners (later ICI, then Dupont). Moreton Valence was sold after the last Javelins had gone, the M5 motorway being built on the line of the runway. Hangar 3 at Hucclecote was demolished around 1991. Gloucestershire Aviation Collection's plans for its Jet Age Museum in Hangar 1 fell through when the whole trading estate was redeveloped as Gloucester Business Park. Simon Gloster Saro ceased production on the estate (at one time occupying the Javelin extension), but a plaque in their foyer commemorating the site's significance in the development of jet aircraft was saved. Only the No. 2 shadow factory remains, with nylon production now under the name Invista.

Moreton Valence reverted in part to farmland, with the remainder being developed as industrial and retail units. The Sunningend works remain in existence as part of

Gloster Javelin aircraft being assembled at the Moreton Valence factory include X756. This was built as an F(AW) Mk 7 variant in June 1958 – one of eighty-five built by Gloster Aircraft. It was returned for conversion to Mk 8 standard in April 1960 and re-designated Javelin F(AW) Mk 9. (Jet Age Museum/Russell Adams Collection)

Lansdown Industrial Estate in Cheltenham. Jet Age Museum's collection was stored until funds were raised for a permanent home near Staverton, which opened to the public in 2013. The plaque from Simon Gloster Saro is displayed in the museum's reception area.

Chapter 4

Component Companies

Aircraft Components Co.

George Dowty (1901–1975) joined Gloucestershire Aircraft Co. (GAC) as a draughtsman in 1924, where Folland was working on the design of the Gamecock fighter. He had previously worked for British Aerial Transport Co., joining them in 1918, and A. V. Roe from 1921. He developed an interest in finding ways to reduce the drag effect of fixed aircraft undercarriages and designed streamline shock-absorbing struts. Dowty also took out a patent for internally sprung landing wheels in 1929, but could not at first interest aircraft manufacturers in his designs. In January 1931, while still working for GAC, he formed the Aircraft Components Co. in the belief that specialised aeroplane parts should be manufactured by independent companies.

Dowty's first order in March 1931 was for a pair of struts for the Cierva C.24 autogiro constructed by de Havilland. Without a workshop of his own, Dowty took on two of Gloster's engineers to do the work. Joe Bowstead carried out machine work on a foot-operated lathe in his cellar, while John Dexter did the fitting and assembly work in a wooden shed in his back garden. In June 1931, the Japanese aircraft company Kawasaki placed an order for six internally sprung wheels, having seen an article on them in *Aircraft Engineering* magazine. Dowty quit Gloster's and set up in a rented mews loft over a wheelwright at 10 Lansdown Terrace, Cheltenham. Apart from a hand-operated pillar drill, only hand tools were available, so Dowty once again turned for help to Bowstead and Dexter as well as subcontracting some of the machine work. The work for Kawasaki was finished by September.

Aircraft Components moved in October 1931 to larger premises, once used by a monumental mason, in Grosvenor Place, Cheltenham; here the first few belt-driven machine tools, together with work benches, were set-up in the single-storey workshop. Dowty continued to secure small orders and in September 1932 the company was registered as Aircraft Components Ltd, with a share capital of £1,000. The workforce rose from five in 1932 to eleven in 1933. The first production contract came from his former employer with an order in 1934 for oleo hydraulic shock absorber struts for twenty-five Gloster Gauntlet aircraft. This was followed, after an unplanned meeting with members of the Bristol design team, by an order for 250 fully castoring self-centring tail wheels for Bristol Bulldog aircraft. By the end of 1934 the company had forty-five employees, had extended the workshops, and had established offices in Bath Street, Cheltenham. The company's first retractable undercarriage was produced for the Heston Type 1 Phoenix five-seat light monoplane. The Dowty Nutcracker retractable undercarriage was also used on the Bristol Type 142 aircraft.

To provide increased production capacity to meet increasing orders, the company purchased Arle Court on the outskirts of Cheltenham in 1935 for £6,000. Accommodation included the 100-year-old Cotswold stone mansion, plus outbuildings, stables, and eight cottages, as well as 100 acres (40.47 hectares) of land upon which workshops and other facilities could be built. Although only offering a small range of aircraft components at this time (with orders worth £5,000 and a workforce of sixty), the company was in a good position to undertake work connected with the imminent expansion of the RAF.

A. W. Martyn (who was previously chairman of H. H. Martyn) provided financial support for the growing company, and he became chairman of Aircraft Components when it was established as a public company in March 1936. The company's name was changed to Dowty Equipment Ltd in 1940 – reflecting an increasing range of products, which included undercarriages, brakes, and wing flaps – and had by then established subsidiaries in Montreal, Canada, and Long Island in the USA.

The Gloster Gladiator had a cantilever undercarriage with internally sprung wheels produced by Dowty. This example from the Shuttleworth Collection was restored in 1953 using the engine from another Gladiator. (M. S. 'Gill' Gillett)

Rotol

By 1933 the Hamilton Standard Propeller Co. of America had patented a variable pitch (v-p) propeller hub. This allowed adjustment of the pitch of the blades during flight to provide full power on take-off and economical high-speed cruising. Gloster Aircraft had been carrying out trials with the British Hele-Shaw Beacham v-p, but Roy Fedden at Bristol Aeroplane Co. had become impatient with the lack of progress in its development and so negotiated terms with the American company. Fedden was unable to gain support from his Bristol directors and de Havilland secured the licence for the Hamilton version. Undeterred, Fedden approached the Air Ministry, which then asked both Bristol Aircraft and Rolls-Royce to produce v-p propellers to the Hele-Shaw design. Fedden was determined to ensure mass production of the best standardised design of v-p propellers and so proposed to Rolls-Royce that they establish a jointly owned company to produce the Hele-Shaw hub. With agreement from the two rival companies, and support from the MoS, Rotol Airscrews Ltd was established in May 1937. The company's name combined elements of the names of the two owning companies.

Rotol set up temporary premises in a former carpet factory near Gloucester's docks. The search for a permanent site followed soon after and negotiations for a new

Rotol's first premises were on Llanthony Road, Gloucester, with the workshops along adjacent High Orchard Street. The site was a vacant lot in 1998 but the refurbished buildings are now part of the Gloucester Quays retail outlet centre. (Author)

factory at Staverton were completed by June 1937. As well as being next to the newly opened RAF airfield, the new factory could tap into an increased potential workforce from Gloucester, Cheltenham, and the newly built housing estate at Churchdown, near Tewkesbury.

By the end of July 1937 all the steelwork for the new Rotol factory had been erected and much of the brickwork also completed. The main contractors for the works were Higgs & Hill of London, while Messrs. Gardiner of Bristol had responsibility for the steelwork of the offices, and Robert Watson had responsibility for the factory steelwork. The contract for constructing a permanent canteen was awarded to W. J. B. Halls of Gloucester in May 1938. The canteen was enlarged after the Second World War.

By the end of 1940 the company had completed 6,000 airscrews and orders had reached 19,200 by 1941. The hydraulically powered v-p hub was at first fitted with magnesium alloy blades, but by 1939 Rotol had changed to using densified wood (timber impregnated with resin and subjected to a high pressure

The office block for Rotol's factory at Staverton was completed by March 1938 and became known as the 'White Block'. It received a planned third storey in 1951, and is now occupied by Safran Landing Systems. (Author)

to increase its strength). Rotol also produced an electrically powered v-p hub under licence from the Curtiss-Wright Corporation in America, but this was discontinued after 1942.

A new office, to bring together all the technical staff, had been built alongside the White Block by January 1943. The £31,000 construction cost was paid for by the MAP. In 1943 the company name was changed to Rotol Ltd, dropping 'Airscrews' to signify that a wider range of aircraft components were being manufactured. The nearby airfield was used extensively by Rotol's flight test department during the Second World War, alongside the Folland and Gloster aircraft companies. During the war, work was carried out at thirty-two dispersal centres, including Gloucester Railway Carriage & Wagon Co. works (repair department); Imperial House, Cheltenham (auxiliaries design office); Roberts Brothers, toy and game makers; Glevum Works, Gloucester (auxiliaries repair department); and factory sites in Worcester (constant speed units), Frome, Somerset (precision and finished parts), Ossett in Yorkshire and Trafford Park, Manchester (wooden blades), and Kilmarnock, Scotland (electric propellers). The workforce at the main factory reached 6,000, who in turn reached a production rate of nearly 500 new or repaired propellers a week. The wartime shortage of metal was alleviated by using laminated wood.

By 1945 around 100,000 airscrews had been produced by Rotol, which had been fitted to over sixty production types of aircraft and forty prototypes. Over 30,000 of these were three-, four- and five-blade constant-speed propellers for Spitfire and Hurricane fighters. Rotol provided the five-blade propellers installed on the world's first turboprop, the Trent-powered Gloster Meteor. Rotol developed a 13-ft (4 m) eight-blade, contra-rotating propeller for the Westland Wyvern multirole strike aircraft – the prototype of which first flew in 1946 – and produced units for all 127 aircraft.

Dowty Equipment

The Dowty company was also kept busy during the Second World War, where up to 3,000 people had been employed, half of them women. The company had been supported by around 250 subcontractors across England and in north America. By the end of the war, Dowty had produced 87,000 landing-gear units. These included 12,900 retracting tail wheels for Hawker Hunter fighter aircraft and 5,000 tail wheel units for Bristol Blenheim aircraft. Dowty constructed landing gear and tail wheels struts in the USA for Australian-built Bristol Beaufort torpedo bombers. Nearly 1 million hydraulic system components were manufactured for 193,515 units. Both the Gloster E28/39 and Meteor jet aircraft were also fitted with Dowty undercarriages.

Apprentices at Bristol Aircraft's technical school are being instructed in the operation of landing gear, which appears to be from a Bristol Beaufort aircraft. Dowty produced undercarriage struts for Beauforts during the Second World War. (Reproduced under licence from and courtesy of BAE SYSTEMS)

Around 1940, Dowty set up an aircraft equipment repair depot at Ashchurch, north of Cheltenham. The Ministry of Supply later built a large single-storey factory alongside this for the repair depot. In December 1947, two new companies were established at this site; Ashchurch Seals Ltd produced synthetic rubber seals, and became Dowty Seals Ltd in November 1949, while Dowty Auto Units Ltd, renamed Dowty Hydraulic Units in August 1954, developed hydraulic industrial applications.

In the early 1950s, facilities at Dowty's Arle Court site included drawing offices, workshops for assembly, machining, plating and polishing, testing rigs, and inspection, maintenance, medical, canteen and recreation blocks. Some 1,500 employees were working on the development of aircraft undercarriages, pumps, and

Above: Dowty's aircraft equipment repair depot at Ashchurch, north of Cheltenham, of 1940 was formerly a Midland Railway forage store for work horses, part of which was used by a custard powder manufacturer. It is seen here in May 1998. (Author)

Below: Dowty manufactured hydraulic struts for the massive undercarriage of the Bristol Type 167 Brabazon airliner. The Dunlop tyres are 62 in. (1.57 m) diameter and 35 in. (0.89 m) wide. (Reproduced under licence from and courtesy of BAE SYSTEMS)

other components for hydraulic systems. Undercarriage drop-test facilities at Arle Court, which included the then largest in the world, were used in the development of the de Havilland Comet airliner, which first entered service in 1952. Other post-war aircraft fitted with Dowty undercarriages included Bristol's Type 167 Brabazon and Type 170 Freighter, and the Avro Vulcan V-bomber. Dowty also supplied the undercarriage, fuel control system, flying controls and high-temperature hydraulics for the Bristol Type 188 research aircraft.

Smiths Aircraft Instruments

S. Smith & Sons (Motor Accessories), manufacturers of speedometers, established in 1915 in Cricklewood, formed its aircraft instruments department in 1929. In 1937 a separate aircraft and marine department, Smiths Aircraft Instruments, was established. This operated with its subsidiary, aircraft instrument makers Henry Hughes & Son. Other products included switches, fire extinguishers, aircraft landing lamps, navigational instruments, automatic pilots, and a wing-tip flare device. In 1939, a site near Cheltenham was identified that would remove the business from anticipated air raids in the London area. The 300-acre (121-hectare) Kayte Farm at Bishop's Cleeve was purchased for £25,000 in April, and S. Smith & Sons (Cheltenham) Ltd was formed in June 1939 as a subsidiary of the main business. Establishment of the factory at Bishop's Cleeve led to the subsequently rapid growth of the village.

A major reorganisation of Smiths was undertaken in 1944, with four divisions comprising motor accessories, industrial instruments, clocks, and aircraft instruments. In 1947 the aircraft instruments division company had 17,000 employees with 2,500 of these at the Cheltenham business. The company name was changed to Smiths Industries in the mid-1960s to reflect its wider product range, which included automotive, marine, and aerospace products.

British Messier

In 1936, Louis Sylvio Armandias (born 1907) came to Britain with a licence from Messier of France to produce landing gear and hydraulic systems. He secured a contract to equip Handley Page Halifax heavy bomber aircraft and, with Rubery, Owen & Co., set-up the Rubery Owen Messier factory at Warrington, then Lancashire. In 1947, after war service, Armandias became co-founder and managing director of British Messier Ltd, with Bristol Aeroplane Co. and Arbo Investments holding equal shares. This new company began operating from wooden huts at the Cheltenham end of Rotol's works.

British Messier relocated to the former Rotol flight test department at Staverton airfield in 1948. Rotol had moved its flight test to Moreton Valence in June 1947, where it shared the large runway with Gloster, and remained until final closure in 1954. Early components produced by the company were hydraulic jacks for operating the dive brakes on the prototype English Electric Canberra jet bomber, which was first flown in 1949. Contracts were subsequently secured to provide undercarriages for the Folland Aircraft Gnat fighter and trainer, and English Electric P.1 research jet aircraft.

In 1949 Rotol acquired Bristol Aeroplane's half-share of British Messier and subsequently the remaining half from Arbo Investments in 1952, thus adding landing

British Messier Ltd supplied landing gear and high-pressure hydraulic systems for the Bristol Type 175 Britannia airliner during the 1950s. (Reproduced under licence from and courtesy of BAE SYSTEMS)

gears to their range of products. The expansion of Rotol's works and offices during 1951 reflected increased demands during the early Cold War period, including the Korean War of 1950–1953. The huts vacated by British Messier in 1948 were replaced with a new building that was at first used as a machine shop, but was later converted to offices. Rotol also produced gearboxes for auxiliary equipment on many British civil aircraft, including the Handley Page Hermes, Avro Tudor, and Bristol Freighter (all introduced from 1945), and the de Havilland Comet, which first flew in 1949. Military aircraft supplied with Rotol components during the same period included the Gloster Meteor and Javelin, as well as aircraft produced by Fairey, Avro, de Havilland, Hawker, and English Electric.

British Messier carried out development work for guided weapons from 1951, including the design and production of rocket motors and pressure bottles. This work was taken over by Bristol Aeroplane Company in 1953 and subsequently Bristol Aerojets, and was not continued beyond 1956. In the late 1950s Rotol attempted to secure work in new markets and a Turbo-Charger Division was formed in August 1957 – later to be renamed the Industrial Division – to serve the commercial road transport market. However, aircraft work continued with British Messier providing undercarriages for Bristol Type 175 Britannia, English Electric Lightning, and Bristol Type 188 aircraft. By 1959 Rotol had also produced 1,600 metallic propeller units for the Vickers Viscount airliner, which had first flown in 1948, and provided the world's first scheduled turboprop airline service, which started in 1952.

Hoffman Bearings

The UK's first ball bearing factory was established in Chelmsford, Essex, in 1898, with funding from American ball bearing machine manufacturer Ernst Hoffman. In anticipation of air raids on the Chelmsford factory (it was in fact attacked several times during the Second World War), a subsidiary factory was opened at Stonehouse, Gloucestershire, in 1938. The site was well placed between the aero-engine factories in Bristol and Derby, and the factory supplied bearings for fighter and bomber aircraft during the war.

In 1969, under Government pressure to consolidate the fragmented UK ball bearing industry, the company became part of Ransomes, Hoffmann & Pollard (RHP). Stonehouse became the aerospace division, manufacturing bearings for engines, gearboxes, and control systems. Bearings for Rolls-Royce Olympus and Pegasus engines built at Bristol were later developed jointly with engineers at the Stonehouse factory.

RHP was purchased by NSK in 1990, with Stonehouse remaining the group's main aerospace facility. In 2002 the factory was acquired by SKF and with MRC (USA) and Avio (Italy) became the aero-engine sub-group. Rolls-Royce continues to be a major customer, with the RB211 and Trent range of engines being equipped with SKF bearings, but it is also a major supplier to Pratt & Whitney and GE. SKF also has a ball bearing factory in Clevedon, Somerset.

Dowty Rotol

When the Dowty Group Ltd was incorporated in March 1954, it had become one of the world's major engineering enterprises, with factories in Canada and Australia. A separate factory at Arle Court was built in 1954 to accommodate the expansion of Dowty Fuel Systems. In 1956 Dowty Hydraulic Units relocated to a large new factory at Ashchurch, which left Dowty Mining Equipment in full occupation of the former MoS building. Dowty Electrics, located at Royal House, Cheltenham, since 1948, moved to a former maltings (built in 1819) near Tewkesbury in 1956.

Rotol was having difficulty in the late 1950s to secure adequate work, which led Bristol Aeroplane and Rolls-Royce to sell their shares to the Dowty Group for £2,235,000 in December 1958. Armandias also left the company in 1958. The new company, Dowty Rotol Ltd, was established in April 1960 and included Rotol's subsidiary British Messier. A programme of rationalisation and relocation followed the takeover. Dowty Equipment moved from Arle Court to Staverton, while Rotol's Industrial Division transferred in turn to Arle Court. All the technical departments were brought together in a refurbished building that had been Rotol's experimental shop. The British Messier factory at Staverton became headquarters for the repair organisation.

The Dowty Fuels factory building at Arle Court had doubled in size by 1961. Products included undercarriages, propellers, hydraulic systems, ram air controls, electrical equipment, and flying controls. In the same year the company acquired Boulton Paul Aircraft Co. at Paddleford Mill Lane, Wolverhampton, to create Dowty Boulton Paul Ltd that, trading as Dowty Aerospace Wolverhampton, manufactured high-technology aero equipment. Through the early 1960s, both the Staverton and Wolverhampton factories were modernised and expanded with new design and production facilities. By 1962, Dowty Rotol employed 13,000 people and had 700 young people undergoing training. The Dowty Rotol subsidiary had annual sales of over £30 million, which accounted for about half of the total business of the Dowty Group. Other subsidiaries manufactured hydraulic seals, as well as mining, marine, and electronics equipment.

Research in the 1960s by Dowty Fuel Systems into digital engine controls resulted in a Bristol Siddeley Pegasus engine being successfully run on a test stand at Staverton in 1978. The company went on to develop fuel control systems for the Hawker Harrier and power controls for Concorde.

In 1968 Dowty Rotol introduced the first fibreglass propellers, which saw widespread use. This was followed in 1980 by the development of carbon fibre composite blades, which offer low weight combined with high strength, are free from corrosion, are resistant to fatigue, and are easy to repair. The Dowty Rotol-equipped Saab 340, the world's first all-composite bladed turboprop aircraft, received certification in 1984. Subsequent developments include constant speed and integrated electronic propeller control systems.

Safran and GE Aviation

Propeller design and manufacture relocated to another part of the Staverton site during the 1990s when the company was split into business units. In 1992 the Dowty Group was acquired by the TI Group (previously Tube Investments). Two years later, TI Group transferred the Dowty landing gear business to a joint venture with French aerospace engine manufacturer SNECMA, which became known as Messier-Dowty. SNECMA later took full control of Messier-Dowty. In 2000 the TI Group merged with Smiths Industries to become the Smiths Group. The twenty-first century began with the propeller business that started as Rotol Airscrews in 1937, absorbed within the Smiths Group. The former Dowty landing gear business was then part of SNECMA.

In 2005 the landing gear manufacturer Messier-Dowty became part of Safran Group with the merger of SNECMA and SAGEM, a French company involved in defence electronics, consumer electronics and communication systems. In 2011 the merger of three Safran subsidiaries (Messier-Dowty, Messier-Bugatti, Messier Services) created Messier-Bugatti-Dowty to become the world's largest manufacturer of fully integrated aircraft landing gear systems. The Dowty name survived until 2016, when the subsidiary was renamed Safran Landing Systems.

The original Dowty Rotol facilities at Staverton, now part of the international Safran Group, accommodate landing gear design, research and systems integration alongside the manufacturing of large complex landing gear structures including main fittings and bogies for large commercial and military aircraft. The Staverton site also has one of the largest landing gear test facilities in the world.

The Smiths Group aerospace division was acquired in 2007 as a subsidiary by GE Aviation, a division of the American conglomerate General Electric. As a result, Dowty Propellers and the former Smiths Industries became part of GE Aviation. Infrastructure developments since this acquisition have included new facilities at the Bishop's Cleeve site, which include an electrical power laboratory and a cockpit simulator.

Dowty Propellers is now a world-leading manufacturer of integrated propeller systems and had delivered 1,000 six-bladed all-composite propellers for the Lockheed Hercules C-130J military transport by 2010. A similar number of propeller assemblies for the Bombardier Dash 8 Q400 regional airliner had been supplied by 2013.

Above: The main landing gears for this all-new Airbus A350-900 jetliner are designed, manufactured and assembled by Safran Landing Systems at Gloucester. (Courtesy Safran Landing Systems)

Below: Dowty Propellers manufacture the propeller system for the Lockheed Martin C-130 J Super Hercules military transport aircraft. Pitch of the swept composite blades is managed by an electronic system integrated with the engine controls. (Adrian Pingstone via Wikimedia Commons)

A fire at Dowty Propeller's production facility at Staverton in early 2015 caused extensive damage to the factory which destroyed its production line. A facility at Vantage Point Business Village in Mitcheldean, Gloucestershire, was selected by parent company GE Aviation as an interim propeller blade manufacturing site and arrangements were made for the redeployment of most of the 230 employees.

The current Dowty Propeller range is used on many turboprop regional airliners such as the Saab 340 and Saab 2000, as well as transport aircraft such as the Leonardo Alenia C-27J Spartan which is fitted with two 13-ft-7-in-diameter (4.15 m), six-bladed propellers. In March 2017, the latest aircraft to be equipped with Dowty Propeller's advanced swept blade R408 propeller system, the Antonov AN-132D multi-purpose transport demonstrator, made its first flight from Kiev in the Ukraine.

Legacy

The region's continuing aerospace industry is the most significant legacy of the aviation business that started out with aeroplanes of wood and fabric more than a century ago. The south-west region of England has one of the largest concentrations of aerospace and defence capabilities in Europe, with a fifth of those working in the UK industry and many more in supply chain businesses. The major businesses at Filton and Patchway continue to preserve and make productive use of buildings from the 1930s and 1940s, alongside modern state-of-the art facilities. The former Brabazon assembly hall and surrounding buildings once used by BAE Systems, however, stand empty or occupied by non-aviation businesses.

Aerospace Bristol at Filton Airfield is both a celebration of past achievements and recognition of the ongoing importance of the industry, as well as being an inspiring insight into the science, technology, and engineering opportunities within aerospace.

The material evidence of this rich aviation heritage is also preserved and interpreted by the Rolls-Royce Heritage Trust, Jet Age Museum, and many other museums and archives. And for the well-informed person, with a keen eye, there are many surviving buildings with aviation associations in Bristol, Gloucestershire, and further afield.

Above: The Bristol engine department's East Works office block of 1936 at Patchway, seen from the Gloucester road in July 1957. (Courtesy of Rolls-Royce Heritage Trust)

Below: Barnwell House at the Airbus Aerospace Park, Filton, seen in February 2015. (Airbus)

Acknowledgements

I am very grateful to the following who read draft text at various stages, often at very short notice, and kindly commented on content and style: Zoe Watson (Archives Manager, Bristol Aero Collection Trust); Bob Hercock (Rolls-Royce Heritage Trust); Chris Bigg, Richard Vernon (Bristol Bloodhound Missile Development Group); Terry Ransome; Vicky Runcie (Media Relations Manager Communications, GDIU, Airbus); Nicholas Britton (Director of Marketing & Communications, Defence Aerospace, Rolls Royce plc); David Hardill (Community Heritage Officer, Yate & District Heritage Centre); John Penny; Tim Kershaw (Jet Age Museum); Peter Hall (Safran Landing Systems); and Laura Dickinson. Several of the above named also provided substantial additional information on particular aspects of the aerospace industry – much more than I could do justice to in this small volume.

The following also kindly provided access to, and granted permission to use, images for which they hold copyright: BAE SYSTEMS; Vicky Runcie (Airbus); Sarah Payne and Robin Cook (Communications Support Officer and Graphic Designer respectively, Defence Aerospace, Rolls-Royce plc); Jane Bradley (Local Studies Librarian, Central Library); and Peter Hall (Safran Landing Systems). Zoe Watson, Bob Hercock, David Hardill and Tim Kershaw also helped me select appropriate images from their respective collections. I am especially grateful to the Bristol Aero Collection Trust, Rolls-Royce Heritage Trust, Yate & District Heritage Centre and Jet Age Museum for access to and use of images from their extensive photograph collections, and am pleased to bring some of this material to a wider audience for the first time. Stephen Laing (Curator, British Motor Industry Heritage Trust) helped to identify motor cars that appear in some of the photographs, and Matt Gillett pointed me in the right direction for some of the current companies in the Bristol area.

Special thanks to Linda Coode (Collections & Exhibition Manager, Bristol Aero Collections Trust) for involving me in the Aerospace Bristol project. My former tutors at the Ironbridge Institute (University of Birmingham), Barrie Trinder, Paul Collins and the late Michael Stratton, also deserve a mention as they first encouraged me to explore the industrial heritage of the aviation industry. And last, but by no means least, my thanks to Connor Stait at Amberley Publishing for his encouragement, guidance, and patience in equal measure!

I have not consulted primary sources to any great extent for the book, but did so when undertaking research for my dissertation, which has been a source of reference in preparing the text. I have made extensive use of published resources, including the relevant 'Putnam Aeronautical Books', which probably remain the best series of single volume references to the products of the manufacturers – *Bristol Aircraft Since 1910* (C. H. Barnes), *Parnall Aircraft Since 1914* (Kenneth E. Wixey) and *Gloster Aircraft Since 1917* (Derek N. James) – though no new editions of these have been published since the 1990s. Tom Rolt's company history *The Dowty Story* was published in 1962, and the 'Archive Photographs Aviation' series *Dowty and the Flying Machine* (Derek N. James) was published in 1996. The 'Archive Photographs' series also include *Bristol Aeroplane Company* and *Gloster Aircraft Company* (both Derek N. James), which were again published some twenty years ago. *Rotol: The History of an Airscrew Company 1937–1960* (Bruce Stait) was published in 1990.

There is of course much information available via the internet, though sadly not all of it is reliable. Most of the current aerospace businesses include a company history on their websites, which has helped to fill out the story of the past quarter century. I have tried to ensure that the information is correct, and not to repeat past errors where I am aware of them, but you don't know what you don't know! I of course take full responsibility for the end result and any remaining errors.

Every attempt has been made to seek permission for copyright material used in this book. However, if we have inadvertently used copyright material without permission or acknowledgement, we apologise and we will make the necessary correction at the first opportunity.